READ AND SHARE®
Bedtime Bible

For:

Lewis

From:

Patrick & Joan

Date:

3/12/14

Give thanks to the Lord and pray to him.
Tell the nations what he has done.
Sing to him. Sing praises to him.
Tell all the wonderful things he has done.
Be glad that you are his.
Let those who ask the Lord for help be happy.
Depend on the Lord and his strength.
Always go to him for help.
Remember the wonderful things he has done.
Remember his miracles and his decisions. . . .
He will keep his promises always.

PSALM 105:1–5, 8

READ AND SHARE®
Bedtime Bible

More Than 200 Bible Stories and 50 Devotionals

Bible Stories Retold by
Gwen Ellis

Illustrated by Steve Smallman and Jeffrey Ebbeler

A Division of Thomas Nelson Publishers

NASHVILLE   DALLAS   MEXICO CITY   RIO DE JANEIRO

Printed in China

12 13 14 15 16 RRD 5 4 3 2 1

www.thomasnelson.com

Bring the *Read and Share® Bedtime Bible and Devotional* to life with the feature-length *Jesus Movie*, available for free streaming for a limited time at:

www.thomasnelson.com/readandsharebedtime

Experience the wonder of the Bible as you are transported to Bethlehem for the story of Jesus' birth. Follow His life and miracles along the shores of the Sea of Galilee, and witness His arrest, crucifixion, and glorious resurrection—all in one dramatic 80-minute movie!

Create an account, and you and your kids can watch this inspiring film for free for a limited time from your computer, smartphone, or tablet!

For Paige and John Mark

Dear Parents

What you are holding in your hands is not just a book; it's a unique way to share God's Word with the children in your life, a way to help them come to know God's love, goodness, and faithfulness to us . . . and to share that good news with others.

In today's fast-paced world, it's not easy to carve out special times together with family. But it's my hope that the 208 bite-size Bible stories and the devotions, divided into two sections in this book, will enable you to make the most out of those important times together.

God bless you and the children in your life as together you get to know Him better through the pages of this book.

Blessings,
Gwen Ellis

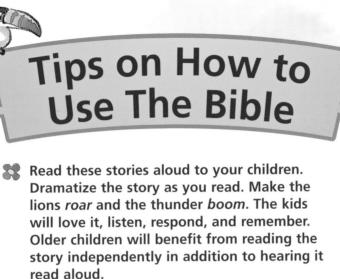

Tips on How to Use The Bible

- Read these stories aloud to your children. Dramatize the story as you read. Make the lions *roar* and the thunder *boom*. The kids will love it, listen, respond, and remember. Older children will benefit from reading the story independently in addition to hearing it read aloud.

- When the story is over, discuss the questions, thoughts, and extra information in the boxes at the end of the stories. These sharing and discussion prompts make this Bible storybook unique, and they help the child to focus on the real meanings of the stories. Don't miss out on this important feature.

- Use the book as a tool to help refresh your memory of favorite stories. You may even hear one you haven't heard before. Either way, embrace it as a learning experience for both you and your child.

- Use *Read and Share® Bible* stories as part of a family Bible study, in Sunday school classes, for bedtime, or for any other special reading time with children.

Bible Contents

New Testament Stories

Devotional Contents

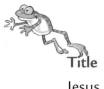

xxi

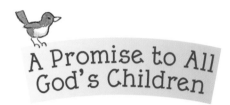

A Promise to All God's Children

"No one has ever seen this.
No one has ever heard about it.
No one has ever imagined
what God has prepared
for those who love him."

1 Corinthians 2:9

Old Testament

The First Day

Genesis 1:1–5

In the beginning God made heaven and earth. At first it was empty and dark. But God gathered up the light and called it *day*.

Then He gathered up the darkness and called it *night*. God was watching over everything.

What do you think God did next?

The Second Day

Genesis 1:6-8

On day two God divided the air from the water. He put some water above the air and some below it. He named the air *sky*.

**The next day God made something many children like,
especially in the summer. Can you guess what it is?**

The Third Day

Genesis 1:9–13

On day three God was busy. He made puddles and oceans and lakes and waterfalls and rivers. He made the dry ground too.

Next He made plants. He made so many different kinds of trees, flowers, and bushes, that no one could count them all. God said His work was good.

Wow! God made so much on that day.
But can you guess what was missing?

The Fourth Day

Genesis 1:14–19

On day four God put the sun in the sky to warm the earth. He saw that the night was very dark, so God put the moon and the stars in the sky.

Then God made spring, summer, fall, and winter. All that He made was good.

9

**Next God made flippy, flappy fun things.
Let's see what they were.**

The Fifth Day

Genesis 1:20–23

On day five God made starfishes, octopuses, whales, and turtles. He made fast little fish for rivers and slippery big fish for the ocean.

He made big birds like eagles to soar in the sky and zippy little birds like hummingbirds. He made birds in all shapes, sizes, and colors.

**Which bird do you think is the prettiest?
Which is the strongest?**

The Sixth Day

Genesis 1:24–31

On day six God made the animals—
puppies, cows, horses, kitties, bears,
lizards, mice, worms, and lots more.
Everything was good.

But something was still missing. There were no people. So God made some. And when He made them, He made them like Himself. He made them so they could be friends with Him.

Where do you think the first people lived?

Adam and Eve

Genesis 2:1–5, 15–22; 3:20

God named the first man Adam. God put Adam in a beautiful garden. He gave him all the animals. He gave him all the fish and the birds too.

Then God gave Adam one more thing.
God made a woman to be Adam's wife.
Adam named his wife Eve. On day seven
God rested from all His work.

**Uh-oh. Something bad was about
to happen on the earth.**

The Sneaky Snake

Genesis 2:16–17; 3:1–6

God gave Adam and Eve one rule. "Eat anything you like except the fruit from the tree in the middle of the garden."

A sneaky old snake came to Eve. "Eat it, then you'll know everything, just like God." So Eve ate the fruit and gave some to Adam. And he ate it too.

When we disobey God, it's called *sin*. There are always consequences when we disobey.

Out of the Garden

Genesis 3:8–24

One evening God came to visit Adam and Eve. But they were hiding. When God found them, He asked, "What have you done?" Adam told God everything. God was sad.

Because they had disobeyed God, Adam and Eve had to leave the beautiful garden. When they were outside of the garden, Adam and Eve had to work very hard to grow food.

**It makes God very sad when we disobey.
It makes our parents sad too.**

Noah

Genesis 6

Many years later there were lots of people on the earth, but most of them were bad. One man—Noah—was good. He obeyed God. "I want you to build a boat," God told Noah.

Noah started right away. People laughed at Noah because they lived in a desert and there was no water for his boat. Noah just went on building the boat.

Do you think it is easy to obey when everyone is laughing at you?

The Big Boat

Genesis 7:1–15

When the boat was finished, God told
Noah and his family to go into the
boat. In went his sons Shem, Ham,
and Japheth. In went their wives and
Mrs. Noah.

"Now bring two of every animal," God told Noah. Noah did exactly what God told him to do. And God watched over him.

23

Something very wet was about to happen outside.

Inside the Boat

Genesis 7:16–24

When the last animal climbed into the boat, God shut the door. *Plip! Plop! Plip!* It began to rain. It rained so much, the water was over the meadows. It rained so much, it covered the towns. It rained so much, it even covered the mountains.

But inside the boat, everyone was safe.

How many days do you think it rained?

The Dove

Genesis 7:12; 8:1–19

After 40 days and 40 nights, the rain stopped, but it still wasn't time to get off the boat. Water was everywhere. One day Noah let a little dove fly out to see what was happening on the earth.

It brought a green leaf back. Hooray!
The plants were growing again! It was
almost time to come out!

**What do you think everyone did when
Noah opened the door of the boat?**

The Rainbow

Genesis 8:18–22; 9:1–17

When everyone was out of the boat, Noah built an altar. He thanked God for keeping them safe. Then something wonderful happened!

God put a beautiful rainbow in the sky and made Noah a promise. "It will never flood over the whole earth like that again," God said. When God makes a promise, He keeps it.

29

All God's promises are in the Bible. Isn't it wonderful to think of all He has promised us?

Babel

Genesis 11:1–9

Many years later there were lots of people on the earth. They all spoke the same language. Some people who lived in the city of Babel became too proud. "Let's build a tower that reaches to the sky. We'll be famous."

God caused them to speak different languages so they couldn't talk to one another. Because they couldn't understand one another, they stopped building the tower.

Do you have any friends who speak a foreign language? Are you patient with them?

Abram

Genesis 12:1–3; 15:5; 22:17

God picked Abram to be the father of a very important family. One day in the future, Jesus would come from this family.

32

God told Abram, "I will make you famous. Your children and grandchildren will be as many as the stars. They will be as many as the grains of sand on the beach. You won't be able to count them."

Wow! That's a wonderful promise. How do you think Abram felt?

Promised Land

Genesis 12:1–9

God told Abram to move to a new place.
Abram had no map. God said, "I will show
you where to go." Abram started out
walking. He took his wife, nephew, and
servants with him.

When Abram and his family got to a land called Canaan, God said, "This is your new home. I am giving it to you and to everyone who will ever be in your family."

If your parents said, "We're going on a trip, but we can't tell you where," would you trust them to take you to a good place?

Abraham's Visitors

Genesis 17:1–8; 18:1–8

When Abram was 99 years old, God changed his name to Abraham. His new name showed that he belonged to God. Not long after that, three men came by Abraham's tent, and he invited them to lunch.

"Quick! Bake some bread," Abraham told his wife. Then Abraham hurried to get some meat cooked. When the food was ready, Abraham brought it to his visitors. The men sat down to eat.

Abraham didn't know it, but his visitors were from heaven.

Sarah Laughs

Genesis 18:9–16

When one of the visitors finished
eating, he said, "Where is your wife,
Sarah?" "She's over there in the tent,"
Abraham said. "Next year Sarah will
have a baby," the visitor said.

Sarah heard and laughed. She couldn't believe it. *I'm too old to have a baby*, she thought. *Abraham is too old too.*

What if your great-grandmother had a baby? Sarah was that old. Let's see how God keeps His promises.

Baby Isaac

Genesis 21:1–7

In about a year Sarah had a baby boy, just like God had promised. Abraham named the baby Isaac. Isaac means "laughter."

Sarah was so happy with her baby boy. She said, "God has made me laugh. Everyone who hears about this will laugh with me."

God can do anything, but sometimes it takes a while to see the answer. What would you like to ask Him to do for you?

A Wife for Isaac

Genesis 24:1–14

Many years later, Isaac was all grown up. "Go back to the land I came from and find a wife for my son," Abraham said to his servant.

The servant loaded up camels with all kinds of wonderful presents. After he got to the land far away, he wasn't sure how to find a wife for Isaac. At a place where girls came to get water, he prayed, "Let the right girl give me water."

How many jugs of water do you think those camels could drink?

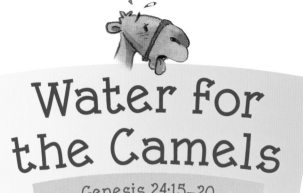

Water for the Camels

Genesis 24:15–20

Before the servant had finished praying, a beautiful young woman came to get water. The servant asked her, "Will you give me some water, please?"

44

"Yes," she said. "I'll get water for your camels too." It was a big job. Thirsty camels can drink a lot of water. Back and forth she went, pouring water for them all.

Do you think the man noticed how kind the woman was?

Rebekah

Genesis 24:21–61

The servant knew this woman was the one to be Isaac's wife. Her name was Rebekah. The servant took gifts to her family and asked if Rebekah could marry Isaac.

Her father said she could, and Rebekah wanted to get married too. So she went home with the servant to meet Isaac.

The servant needed God to help him find the right girl. What do you do when you need God's help?

Isaac and Rebekah

Genesis 24:62-67

The camels swayed and bumped along the road all the way to Canaan where Isaac lived. One evening just before the sun went down, the camels stopped.

48

A young man was walking in the field. He looked up and saw the camels. His bride had come. Isaac loved Rebekah. He married her.

Do you think Rebekah was excited about being chosen to be Isaac's wife? How do you think she felt about going so far away?

The Twins

Genesis 25:21–26

For many years Rebekah couldn't have babies. So Isaac prayed to God about the problem. God heard Isaac, and He sent *two* babies—twins. When the twins were born, one was all red and fuzzy. Isaac and Rebekah named him Esau.

The other twin had smooth skin. They named him Jacob. Someday, when they were grown up, these boys would be the leaders of two great families.

God has the answers to all our prayers.
What would you like to pray about?

Sneaky Jacob

The boys grew up, and one day Esau came in from hunting. Jacob was cooking. "I'm hungry. Give me some of that soup!" said Esau.

52

Jacob was a sneaky guy. He said, "Give me your rights as the firstborn son, and I will." Esau agreed, "Okay. If I starve, my rights won't help me."

Esau made a bad decision. Pray and ask God to help you make good decisions.

Foolish Esau

Genesis 25:34; 27:1–37

Jacob gave Esau a big bowl of soup, and he ate it. Esau didn't even know he had been tricked.

Later on Esau found out what that bowl of soup cost him. Isaac, their father, gave everything he had to Jacob when it should have been Esau's. Esau had been foolish.

Esau thought he had to have something right now. Why is it foolish *not* to think about consequences?

A Ladder to Heaven

Genesis 27:41–46; 28:10–18

When Esau found out how Jacob had tricked him, he was mad. Jacob was afraid and ran away from him. That night in the desert, Jacob had to sleep outside with a rock under his head for a pillow.

56

He dreamed about a ladder to heaven filled with angels. God spoke to Jacob in the dream and promised to bless him.

57

What do you think it would be like to have a rock for a pillow?

Rachel

Genesis 29:1–20

Jacob continued his journey, traveling
a long way to his uncle Laban's house.
There he met Laban's beautiful daughter
Rachel. Jacob fell in love with her.

He told Laban, "I'll stay here and work for you if you'll let me marry Rachel." So Jacob stayed and worked seven years for the woman he loved.

59

Is there anything you'd be willing to wait seven years for?

Tricked!

Genesis 29:21–24

After seven years of hard work, it was finally time for Jacob's wedding. Everyone got dressed. The bride wore a heavy veil over her face. It was so heavy that Jacob couldn't see through it.

Guess what? Laban tricked Jacob. Rachel was not under the veil. It was her sister, Leah, instead.

How do you think Jacob felt when he found out he had been tricked?

Home Again

Genesis 29:25–30; 31:1–55

Jacob was mad at Laban. "What have you done?" Jacob asked. Laban said, "Work some more, and I'll give you Rachel too." Jacob married Rachel and worked seven more years.

Then Jacob decided to leave Rachel's sneaky father. He took his family and everything he had and started back home.

Jacob was going home, but that's where his angry brother, Esau, lived. What do you think happened when they met?

Jacob Wrestles with God

Genesis 32:26–28

When Jacob was almost home, a servant said, "Your brother, Esau, is coming." Jacob thought Esau was coming to hurt him. Jacob was afraid and prayed, "God, save me from my brother!"

That night a man, who was really God, appeared. Jacob wrestled with the man. "Bless me," Jacob said. God blessed Jacob and changed his name to Israel.

Jacob means "sneaky." *Israel* means "one who wrestles with God." Which kind of person would you rather be?

Jacob and Esau Meet

Genesis 33

The next morning Esau came. Jacob bowed in fear in front of him. Surprise! Esau was happy to see Jacob. Esau ran to Jacob and gave him hugs and kisses.

"Who are all these people?" Esau asked. "They are mine," Jacob answered. "God has been good to me." The brothers became friends again.

Do you have brothers and sisters?
Do you treat them kindly?

Joseph's Dreams

Genesis 37:1–8

Jacob had 12 sons. He loved them all, but he loved Joseph best. Joseph liked to tell his brothers about his dreams. He said, in one dream, all 12 brothers had bundles of wheat.

Then he said 11 bundles bowed down to his bundle. Oooo! That made the older brothers mad. "You're not the king over us," they told him.

God had a plan for this family that no one could see yet. God has a plan for your family too.

Joseph's Coat

Genesis 37:3, 12–20

Jacob gave Joseph a beautiful coat with long sleeves. This made his brothers jealous.

One day Jacob said, "Joseph, go check on your brothers." So off Joseph went. His brothers saw him coming. "Here comes the dreamer," they said. "Let's get rid of him." Watch out, Joseph!

**Those brothers were up to no good.
What would they do to Joseph?**

Joseph Is Sold

Genesis 37:21-28

The brothers hated Joseph. But one of them said, "Let's not hurt him. Let's just throw him down this well." He planned to rescue Joseph later. So they took off Joseph's coat and threw him in.

About that time, some men on camels rode by. "Hey," the brothers said, "let's sell him to be a slave." They sold their own brother.

**What the brothers did was awful.
What would happen next?**

Joseph the Slave

Genesis 39:1-6

Joseph was not alone. God was watching
over him. Soon a rich man named Potiphar
bought him to be his slave. Joseph worked
and did great at everything Potiphar
asked him to do.

So Potiphar put Joseph in charge of his whole house, and everyone had to do what Joseph said.

Even when things look bad, God is watching over His children. He's watching over you right now.

Joseph in Jail

Genesis 39:6–20

Everything was going great for Joseph, until one day Potiphar's wife tried to trick him. She told lies about Joseph, and Potiphar believed her.

Potiphar threw Joseph into jail. Poor Joseph. His brothers sold him, a lady lied about him, and he was thrown into jail. It wasn't fair. But God had a plan for Joseph.

Lots of things happen to us that aren't fair. But, remember, God always has a plan to help us.

Joseph Explains Dreams

Genesis 40:1–13, 20–21

In the prison, one of the prisoners told
Joseph about a dream he'd had. Joseph
listened carefully, and God showed him
what the man's dream meant.

Joseph said that in three days the man would be working for the king of Egypt like he had before being put in prison. Sure enough, that's exactly what happened.

Joseph knew what God could do. He had learned how to listen to God. You can too.

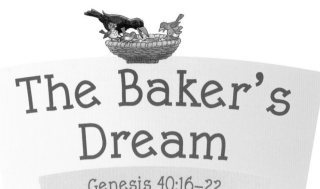

The Baker's Dream

Genesis 40:16-22

Another prisoner dreamed he had three baskets of bread that he had baked for the king. In his dream the birds kept eating up all the bread.

Joseph didn't have very good news about this dream. He said, "In three days you will die." Joseph told the truth.

Why do you think Joseph was so good at telling what dreams meant? The most important dream Joseph would hear about was just ahead.

The King's Dream

Genesis 41:1–36

One night the king of Egypt dreamed that seven skinny cows came from the river and ate up seven fat cows. No one could figure out what the dream meant.

"Call for Joseph," said the first man who had told Joseph his dream in the prison. They did, and God showed Joseph what the king's dream meant. There would be seven years with lots of food. Then there would be seven years with almost no food.

That was a scary dream, wasn't it? Sometimes our dreams mean something, and sometimes they are just dreams.

83

Joseph
in Charge

Genesis 41:37–43

When the king heard what Joseph said,
he did something amazing. He put Joseph
in charge of gathering enough food to
feed everyone during the hungry time.

The king took off his royal ring and put it on Joseph's finger. He gave Joseph fine clothes to wear and put a gold chain around his neck. The king had Joseph ride in one of the royal chariots, and everyone had to bow down to him.

Joseph went from being a prisoner in the morning to a ruler in the afternoon. That was because God had a plan for Joseph and his family.

Joseph's Brothers Visit Egypt

Genesis 41:46–42:6

For the next seven years, Joseph stored lots of food. Then the hungry time came. It was bad for other lands, but the people of Egypt had food.

Joseph's family, back home, were very hungry. "Go to Egypt and buy grain," Jacob told his sons. So ten brothers packed up and went to Egypt. The youngest brother, Benjamin, stayed home.

Whoa! What do you think the brothers will do when they see Joseph?

Spies!

Genesis 42:7–20

When the brothers came to the palace,
Joseph knew right away who they were.
But they didn't recognize him.

"You're spies," he said to test them. They replied, "No, we've come to buy food." They told Joseph all about their family.

Joseph gave them food but said if they ever came back they must bring their youngest brother.

Joseph wanted to see Benjamin. What do you think the brothers were thinking? Do you think they'll bring Benjamin next time?

89

The Bowing Brothers

Genesis 43:15–26

One day Joseph's brothers needed more food. They came back to Egypt and brought Benjamin with them. Joseph told his servants to prepare a feast for them.

When Joseph came to the feast, all the brothers bowed down to him. It was just like Joseph's dream about his brothers' bundles of wheat bowing down to his.

Do you think Joseph's dream had come true?

Joseph Tricks His Brothers

Genesis 43:29–44:13

When Joseph saw Benjamin, he was so happy, he began to cry. But he didn't let anyone see his tears. Joseph gave the brothers the grain they wanted.

But he tricked them. He put his cup in Benjamin's sack. The rule was that whoever took something from the ruler had to be his servant forever. Benjamin couldn't go home.

Joseph tricked his brothers because he wanted to see if their hearts had changed or if they would let someone take another brother.
What would happen next?

Jacob Goes to Egypt

Genesis 44:3–45:28

The brothers begged Joseph not to keep
Benjamin. Joseph saw that their hearts
had changed. He said, "I am your brother
Joseph. You sold me to be a slave, but
God sent me here to save your lives."

"Hurry, go home and get our father and your families and bring them here." And that's how God's people, the Israelites, came to live in Egypt.

God always has a plan. He has a plan for you too.

A Mean King

Exodus 1:8–14

Years later, long after Joseph died, a mean king made the Israelites his slaves. The slave masters were mean too. They made the Israelites work harder and harder to make bricks and do other things for the king.

"There are too many Israelites, and they are too strong," said the king. So he thought up an awful thing to do.

Why do you think the king was mean to the Israelites?

A Baby Boy

Exodus 1:22–2:2

That mean old king said, "Every time an Israelite baby boy is born, you must throw him into the river." That was terrible!

One day an Israelite woman had a beautiful baby boy. She decided to hide her baby from the evil king and his helpers. It was a good choice.

When we make the right choice, God always helps us. Let's see what happened next.

The Good Sister

Exodus 2:3–4

After a while the baby's mother couldn't hide him anymore. So she got a basket and fixed it so the water could not get inside.

Then she put the baby into the basket and put the basket into the river. The baby's big sister, Miriam, stayed close by to see what would happen.

Miriam must have been very frightened. What do you think she said when she prayed for her little brother?

A Princess Finds Moses

Exodus 2:5–10

God was watching over the baby. When the princess came to the river to take a bath, she saw the basket. "Go get that basket," she told her servant.

The princess looked inside the basket. Just then the baby cried, and she felt sorry for him. The princess decided to keep him as her son. She named him Moses.

This was exciting! Moses was going to be a prince of Egypt. But something even better was about to happen.

Moses' Real Mother Helps

Exodus 2:7–10

Miriam was still watching. Even though she was frightened, she stepped out and asked, "Do you need someone to take care of the baby?" The princess smiled. "Why, yes," she replied.

Miriam ran home and got her mother—
Moses' own mother—to take care of
him. God saved Baby Moses and gave
him back to his mother for a long time.

**Many exciting things were going to happen
to Moses when he grew up. Let's read on.**

Moses Runs Away

Exodus 2:11–3:3

After a while Moses went to the palace to live. When he was grown up, Moses did something very bad. He killed another man.

Moses ran away to live in the desert. He married a lady named Zipporah. Her father's name was Jethro. One day when Moses was out with the sheep, he saw a bush in the desert. It was on fire, but it didn't burn up.

What was going on? Why didn't the bush burn up?

Strange Fire

Exodus 3:4–12

Moses went to look at this strange fire. God spoke to Moses from the fire. "Don't come any closer. Take off your sandals. You are on holy ground." Moses was scared. He covered his face. "Go, bring My people out of Egypt," God said.

"I can't do that," Moses said. But God promised to help Moses lead the people.

109

Whenever God asks us to do hard things, He will help us. Let's see how He helped Moses.

Moses Goes Home

Exodus 4:14–5:1

Moses went home to Egypt to talk to the Israelites about being free. God sent Moses' brother Aaron to help him.

The Israelites fell right down on their knees and thanked God for remembering them. Then it was time for Moses to go see the mean king. Moses took Aaron with him.

Oh my! Moses had to ask the king to let all those people go free. What do you think the king said?

The King Says No!

Exodus 5:1–9

Moses walked right up to the king and said, "God says, 'Let My people go!'" The king said, "I don't know your God. Why should I obey Him? These people have work to do. They cannot leave."

Then the king made the people work even harder. What a mean man! This made the Israelite leaders angry with Moses.

Do you think Moses had made a mistake?

A Mistake?

Exodus 5:19–6:9

The Israelite leaders were angry. They thought Moses had surely made a big mistake. "You made the king hate us," they said.

Moses talked to God. "Lord, why have You brought this trouble on the people? Is this why You sent me here?" God answered, "You will see what I will do to the king."

Sometimes even when we do good, things get worse for a while. This is when we need to remember that God can see ahead.

The Walking-Stick Miracle

Exodus 7:8–13

God sent Moses and Aaron back to the king. "Let God's people go," Moses said. "Do a miracle," said the king. Aaron threw down his walking stick, and it became a snake.

The king's magicians threw down their sticks, and they became snakes too. But Aaron's snake swallowed them all. God's power was the strongest. Still the king was so evil and his heart was so hard that he said, "No, your people cannot leave."

This is just getting harder and harder. How will God rescue His people?

A River Turns to Blood

Exodus 7:14–24

God said to Moses, "Go meet the king at the river. Tell him to let My people go, or I will turn this river into blood." Of course, the king said no. So Aaron hit the water with his walking stick, and the river turned to blood.

It smelled awful, and there was no water for the people to drink.

Sometimes people don't want to listen to God. What else do you think will happen to that stubborn king?

Frogs, Frogs, Frogs

Exodus 7:25–8:15

After seven days Moses went back to the king. "Let God's people go," said Moses. "No," said the king.

120

This time God sent frogs. Not just one or two, but more than anyone could count! The frogs went in the houses, in the beds, in the food, and in the ovens. The frogs were icky, and they were everywhere.

God meant business. How much worse do you think it will get before the king says yes?

Gnats, Flies, and Boils

Exodus 8:16–9:12

Every time the king said no, things just went from bad to worse in Egypt. God sent little bitty gnats that crawled all over the people.

Next He sent millions of flies. They were everywhere. Cows got sick and died. Then people got sick with big sores called *boils*. But the king still said no each time.

That king sure was stubborn! Can you guess what awful thing came next?

Hail, Locusts, and Darkness

Exodus 9:13–10:29

Next God sent a storm. Big chunks of ice called *hail* pounded every plant into the ground. Then hungry grasshoppers called *locusts* blew in with the wind. There were so many of them, the people couldn't see the ground. The grasshoppers ate all the food.

124

Then God sent darkness right in the middle of the day. The Egyptians couldn't see anything. But the king still said no.

Why do you think the king kept saying no?

Standing-Up Dinner

Exodus 11:1–12:28

God told His people to fix a dinner of roast lamb and to eat dinner standing up with all their clothes on.

He told them to have their walking sticks in their hands. God knew the king would soon change his mind, and His people needed to be ready to go.

On this night the children got to stay up late and eat dinner with their parents. Tell what you think happened next.

Something Awful

Exodus 12:29–51

At midnight because the king was so stubborn, something awful happened in Egypt. All the oldest boys, cows, horses, and other animals died. But not one of God's people or their animals died.

128

Finally the king said, "Take everything you have and leave Egypt." God's people were free at last!

God doesn't want bad things to happen to people, but He had to make the king listen.

Cloud and Fire

Exodus 13:21-22

When God's people left Egypt, they marched out into the desert. God did something very special to help them. He sent a tall cloud to guide them during the day.

It was very dark in the desert at night.
So God changed the cloud to fire. It was
like a giant night-light. Now God's people
could travel some during the day and
some at night.

**God loved His people. He was taking care of them
just like He takes care of us.**

Trapped at the Red Sea

Exodus 14:5–14

Back in Egypt the king changed his mind. He sent his army after the Israelites to bring them back. Closer and closer the army of horses and chariots came.

God's people stood right by the Red Sea. There was no way across the water. The king's soldiers were behind them, and the sea was in front of them. It looked as if they were trapped, but they weren't.

How do you think God's people felt at that moment? Sad? Scared? Hopeful?

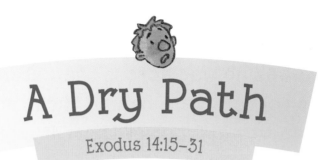

A Dry Path

Exodus 14:15–31

Just then God moved the tall cloud behind His people to hide them from the enemy. The Egyptians couldn't see anything. The cloud made it dark for them. But it gave light to God's people on the other side of the cloud.

Then Moses raised his hand over the sea. All night God pushed back the sea with a strong wind. And the water split to make a dry path to the other side. The Israelites safely reached the other side. But when the Egyptian army tried to use the same path, the water came back together and covered the soldiers. And that was the end of the king's army.

Can you imagine what it was like to walk on a path in the middle of the sea?

Food and Water

Exodus 15:22–17:7

God led His people through the desert.
God loved them. He made sure they had
plenty of food and water. He gave them
a strange, white food called *manna*. It
came from the sky and was very good
for them, but the people whined and
whined.

Once God even made water come out of a rock so they would have fresh water to drink. The people were happy to have water. They stopped whining for a little while.

God wants us to be thankful. What are you thankful for? What should you tell God?

Ten Commandments

Exodus 20:2–17; 24:12–18

One day God called Moses up to the top of a mountain to have a talk.

138

God gave Moses many rules to help His people know how to live. God wrote the rules on stone with His finger. We call these rules *The Ten Commandments*.

God gives us rules to keep us safe. Rules help us live happy lives. Moms and dads have rules too. Can you name one?

A Tent House for God

Exodus 25:8–9; 31:1–11

God had told Moses to build a Holy Tent so that God could live close to His people. Then God gave Moses someone to help him build the Holy Tent.

The helper's name was Bezalel. God said His Spirit would help Bezalel know how to make beautiful things from silver and gold and jewels and carved wood for God's house.

God gives different skills and talents to different people. What do you do best? Have you thanked God for this special talent?

A Holy Box

One of the things Bezalel made for the Tent was the Holy Box. He covered the box with pure gold. He made a lid of pure gold too.

Moses put the stones with God's commandments on them inside the Holy Box. Bezalel and Moses worked hard to make everything perfect. When the Holy Tent was finished, God's presence filled it up. God had come to live with His people.

Where do people go to worship God today?

Moses and Joshua

Exodus 33:7–11

Before the Holy Tent was built, Moses would set up another tent outside the camp. When Moses went to the tent to talk with God, he often took a young man named Joshua with him.

All the people stood outside and watched the two men go by. As soon as Moses and Joshua were inside the tent, the tall cloud would come down and cover the doorway.

What do you suppose was going on inside the tent? Let's see.

Inside the Tent

Exodus 33:11; Joshua 1:1–9

Inside the tent God and Moses talked like old friends, and Joshua listened. This was one of the ways Moses was teaching Joshua how to be a leader of God's people.

146

When Moses left the tent to go home,
Joshua liked to stay at the tent.

It was important for Joshua to get to know God.
God had lots of work for him to do.

You can get to know God, too, by praying and
listening to what God says in the Bible.

Moses Sees God

Exodus 33:18–23; 34:29–35

One day Moses asked God, "Will You show me how great You are?" God tucked Moses into a crack in a rock and passed in front of him.

Moses only saw God's back. But it was enough. Moses' face became so shiny from being close to God that people couldn't look at him. Moses had to cover his face to keep the light from hurting their eyes.

Wow, Moses really got close to God, didn't he? How do you think we can get close to God?

12 Men Explore

Numbers 13:1–14:35

One day Moses sent 12 men to explore the land God had promised His people. The land had lots of food, but the people who lived there were like giants. Two men, Joshua and Caleb, said, "Don't worry. God is with us, and He is stronger than any giants."

But the other men were afraid and said, "We can't go into the land." God was not happy with His people. They did not trust Him. So God's people had to wander around in the desert 40 more years.

God wants us to believe His Word. Of the 12 men who explored the new land, who were the two that trusted God?

151

Balaam's Donkey

Numbers 22:1–22

Close to the end of their time in the desert, all God's people camped near a city. The king of that city was afraid when he saw so many people camped nearby. He sent for a prophet named Balaam. "Do something to make these people go away," he said.

So Balaam started off on his donkey to see what he could do. That made God angry because He wanted His people to be there.

God had a big surprise for Balaam. Turn the page and see what happened.

The Donkey and the Angel

Numbers 22:22–35

God sent an angel with a sword to stop
Balaam. Balaam couldn't see the angel,
but his donkey could. The donkey stopped.
When Balaam beat the donkey to make it
go, the donkey said, "Why are you beating
me?" Then Balaam saw the angel. The
angel told Balaam to help God's people.

**God can do anything. He even made a donkey
talk so Balaam would pay attention.**

Crossing Jordan

Joshua 3

Finally it was time for God's people to go into their new land. But first they had to cross the Jordan River.

156

There were no bridges or boats. God told the priests to carry the Holy Box and walk into the water. When they did, God made a dry path, and His people walked across to the other side of the river.

157

What do you think other people thought when they heard what God did for His people?

The Walls of Jericho

Joshua 6

The first city they came to was Jericho. It had huge walls and gates and guards everywhere. God said, "March around Jericho every day for six days. Seven priests with trumpets must march at the front."

"On the seventh day, march around seven times. Then have the priests blow one long blast on their trumpets. The people must shout and the walls will fall down." The people obeyed and down came those walls.

Sometimes God asks us to do things we don't understand. We just need to obey.

The Sun Stands Still

Joshua 10:1–14

Joshua fought hard to win the land
God had promised to His people. And
God helped him. One day God sent huge
hailstones to fall on the enemy.

Later that day the battle was not finished. Joshua said, "Sun, stand still!" God kept the sun right where it was until His people won the battle.

Nothing is impossible when God is on our side. God wants to help us.

Deborah

Judges 4:1–16

When the people got settled in their new land, God gave them leaders to help them. One of them was a woman named Deborah. People came to her under a tree, so that she could settle their arguments.

She and her general, Barak, went into battle. Deborah was a brave woman who could win against their enemies. God was on her side.

Deborah was only one of many brave leaders. Let's see who else was a leader.

Gideon

Judges 6:11–24

One day an angel came to a man named Gideon. The angel said, "The Lord is with you, mighty warrior! Go save God's people."

164

Gideon said, "Not me. My family is the weakest in our tribe, and I am the weakest in our family." The angel said to Gideon, "I will be with you." And that's how Gideon became a leader of God's people.

God doesn't always look for the strongest person to do His work. He looks for people who will do what He asks them to do.

Too Many Soldiers

Judges 6:33–7:8

166

Gideon was scared, but he decided he would do what God asked. He got an army together. God said, "You have too many soldiers." Gideon sent thousands of men home. God said, "You still have too many. Take them to drink water. Keep only those who put water in their hands and lap it like a dog." That left Gideon with only 300 soldiers.

How could Gideon win a war with only 300 soldiers? Just see what God does next!

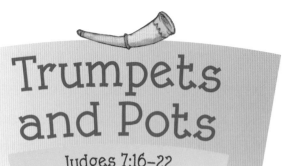

Trumpets and Pots

Judges 7:16–22

God told Gideon to give each of his men trumpets and jars. A burning torch was inside each jar.

While the enemy was sleeping, Gideon's men blew their trumpets as loudly as they could. Then they broke their pots and let the fire from the torches shine. The enemy soldiers woke up, and they were so scared they began fighting one another. After a while they ran away.

Because Gideon did what God told him to do, God won the battle for His people! Yea, God!

Samson

Judges 13:1–5, 24–25

One of the leaders of God's people was chosen before he was born.

An angel told the mother, "You will have a son! But you must never cut his hair. His long hair will show that he's a Nazirite—someone who has work to do for God."

This baby grew up to be very strong. His name was Samson, and he always won against his enemies.

It's too bad Samson wasn't as smart as he was strong. He was about to get in a bunch of big trouble.

Samson's Haircut

Judges 16:4–21

Samson had a girlfriend. Her name was Delilah. She asked, "What makes you so strong, Samson?" At first he wouldn't tell her. She begged and whined. Finally he said, "If someone shaved my head, I would lose my strength."

When Samson fell asleep, Delilah had someone to shave off his hair. Samson wasn't strong anymore. Now his enemies had no trouble taking him to their prison.

Poor Samson. He wasn't wise when he chose Delilah to be his friend. We need to be careful about the kind of friends we choose.

Pushing the Pillars

Judges 16:23–31

In prison Samson's hair grew long again. One night his enemies had a party. They brought Samson in and made fun of him.

174

Samson asked God to help him once more. And God did. When Samson pushed against the pillars that held up the building, down it all came on top of everyone. Those people would never hurt anyone again.

175

**Samson was the strongest man in the Bible.
Who made him strong?**

Ruth and Naomi

Ruth 1

Ruth and Naomi were widows. That means their husbands had died. Ruth had been married to Naomi's son. One day Naomi decided to go back to the land from which her family had come.

Ruth decided to go with her. Naomi thought Ruth might miss her family and friends. She told Ruth not to come with her. But Ruth said, "Don't ask me to leave you!" And so they went together.

Ruth didn't know where she was going, and she didn't know the big surprise waiting for her. Try to guess what it was.

Ruth Gathers Grain

Ruth 2

Ruth and Naomi were very poor. They didn't have enough to eat. Naomi was too old to work, so Ruth went out to a rich man's field to gather leftover grain for food. The rich man saw her. She was a beautiful young woman. "Stay here and work in my field," he told her.

Ruth was taking care of Naomi, and God was taking care of them both. But God wasn't finished with His surprise yet. What will it be?

179

Ruth and Boaz

Ruth 3–4

Naomi decided Boaz would be a good husband for Ruth. She told Ruth what she should do to see if Boaz wanted to marry her. Ruth did exactly what Naomi said. Boaz liked Ruth and wanted to marry her. So they were married and had a little boy. That made all of them happy.

God's surprises are always very special if we can just wait for His time to give them to us.
Tell about a surprise you've had.

Hannah's Prayer

1 Samuel 1:1–18

One day a woman named Hannah went to God's Holy Tent to pray. She asked God for a baby son. She promised God her son would work for Him all his life. Eli, the priest, saw her praying. He thought there was something wrong. Hannah told him she was very sad and talking to God about her troubles. Eli said, "May the Lord give you what you want." Hannah was not sad anymore.

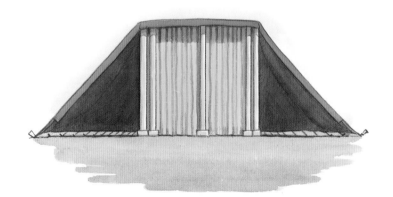

183

What do you pray to God about?

Hannah's Boy

1 Samuel 1:19–28; 2:19

Hannah's prayer was answered. She had a baby boy and named him Samuel, which means "God heard."

When Samuel was about three years old, Hannah took him to Eli, the priest at the Holy Tent. Hannah loved Samuel very much. Every year she made him a new coat.

Hannah kept her promise to God by taking Samuel to Eli. God had big plans for Samuel. What do you think they were?

Samuel Listens

1 Samuel 3:1–14

Samuel's job was to help Eli in the Lord's work. One night Samuel ran to where Eli the priest was sleeping. Samuel had heard someone call his name, and he thought it was Eli. "I didn't call you," Eli said. "Go back to bed."

So Samuel went back to bed, but the voice called him two more times. After the third time, Eli knew that God was calling Samuel. Eli told Samuel to say, "Speak, Lord. I'm listening." God told Samuel that He was going to punish Eli's sons because they were evil.

What would you do if God called you in the middle of the night?

Losing the Holy Box

1 Samuel 4

When Samuel had grown up, there was a war. God's people decided to take the Holy Box into the battle. When they did this, they did not follow God's rules. Guess what? The enemy captured the Holy Box of God and took it home with them. God's people were sad.

God's people knew the rules, but
decided not to follow them.
What do you think about following rules?

189

Coming Home

1 Samuel 5–6:13

As soon as the enemy got the Holy Box of God home, bad things started happening to them. They wanted to get rid of it. They put the Holy Box in a cart pulled by two cows and sent it home. When God's people saw the Holy Box coming, they were so happy!

God's people didn't even have to fight to get the Holy Box back. God will take care of us, even when someone is mean to us.

A Scary Thunderclap

1 Samuel 7:2–11

The enemy wasn't quite through yet.
They saw God's people meeting together
and decided to attack them. The people
begged Samuel to pray. He did, and God
sent a thunderclap so loud it frightened
the enemy soldiers. Then God's people
chased them away.

193

Wow! That must have been quite a thunderclap.
God can even use nature to win over evil.

A King for Israel

After a while God's people decided they wanted a king. God didn't think that was a good idea, but He told Samuel to pour oil on the head of a tall, young farmer named Saul. That showed God had chosen him to be king.

194

At first Saul let Samuel help him make good decisions. But then Saul decided to do things that made God unhappy. So God decided to let someone else be king in Saul's place. It made Samuel sad to tell Saul that God didn't want him to be king anymore.

Isn't it too bad about Saul? Let's see who God chose to be the next king.

The Youngest Son

1 Samuel 16:1–13

God sent Samuel to the house of a man named Jesse to choose a new king. When Samuel looked at seven of Jesse's sons, God said to him, "Don't look at how tall or handsome they are."

"Are these all of your sons?" Samuel asked. Jesse said, "My youngest son is taking care of the sheep. His name is David." God said to Samuel, "David is the one I've chosen."

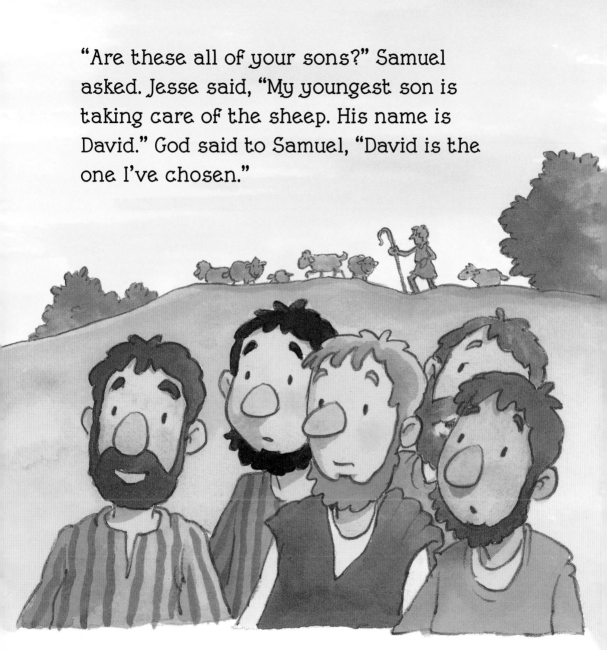

God doesn't care if you are tall or short or have blue eyes or brown. He just wants you to have a heart that loves Him.

David the Shepherd

1 Samuel 16:11; Psalm 23

David was a shepherd. It was his job to protect and care for sheep. When he was with the sheep, he made up songs and sang them to God. One of those songs says: "The Lord is my shepherd. I have everything that I need."

As David watched the sheep, he became close friends with God.

It's good to sing songs to God.
What is your favorite song to sing to Him?

David and the Giant

1 Samuel 17:1–24

God's Holy Spirit came to be with David. It made him brave and strong. One day Jesse told David to go check on his brothers who were soldiers. When David got to the battlefield, he found the soldiers were all afraid of a giant named Goliath. Goliath liked to yell at the soldiers and scare them. He wanted to hurt them.

God gave David courage so he wouldn't be afraid of the giant. What would you do if you needed some courage?

Down Goes the Giant

1 Samuel 17:25–58

David wasn't afraid of Goliath. He gathered five smooth small stones and put them in his pouch. Then with his slingshot in one hand, David went to meet Goliath.

The giant laughed when he saw that David was just a boy. But David shot a stone from the slingshot. It hit Goliath in the head and killed him.

David was brave, and he trusted God. God will help us in scary times if we just ask Him.

King Saul Chases David

1 Samuel 18–23

By killing the giant Goliath, David became a hero. God's people loved him. King Saul became jealous of David and eventually tried to kill him. Saul and his soldiers chased after David and hunted for him everywhere.

But David and the brave men who went with him were protected by God, and Saul couldn't catch them.

Let's see how David gets away from Saul. You may be surprised.

David and Jonathan

1 Samuel 18:1–4; 20

King Saul had a son named Jonathan. Jonathan was a prince. He and David were best friends. He even gave David his coat. Jonathan knew his father wanted to hurt David. So Jonathan helped David run away and hide from Saul. That was a brave thing for Prince Jonathan to do. If David became the next king, Jonathan would never be king of Israel.

Best friends help each other. Do you have a best friend? What could you do to help your friend?

Jonathan's Son

1 Samuel 31; 2 Samuel 1:1–11; 5:1–4; 9

One day King Saul and his son Jonathan died in a battle against the enemy. When David heard this, he was very sad. Soon afterward, David became king. He always took care of his best friend Jonathan's son Mephibosheth. Mephibosheth was crippled in both feet.

David loved God and wanted to please Him.
But one time David made a big mistake.
Let's see what happened.

209

David Does Wrong

2 Samuel 11–12:13; Psalm 51

David usually went to war with his soldiers. But one time he stayed home and got into big trouble. He took another man's wife as his own. The woman's name was Bathsheba. Then David sent the man into battle to be killed. That was wrong!

When David realized how wrong he had
been, he was truly sorry. He asked God
to forgive him, and God did.

**God will forgive us if we are truly sorry for what
we've done wrong and ask His forgiveness.**

A Wise Woman

2 Samuel 20:1, 14–22

Joab, David's general, and the
army were trying to catch
a troublemaker. They were
digging under the wall of a
city to make it fall down. Then
a wise woman inside the city
called down to Joab, "What are
you doing?"

"We're trying to capture a troublemaker," Joab said. The wise woman told the city leaders that there was a troublemaker hiding in their city. So the leaders captured and killed the bad man. When Joab heard this, he took his army and went home. The city was saved.

We don't even know this lady's name, but we remember her because she was brave.

The Wisest Man

1 Kings 3:4–15

David was king for forty years.
He had many sons. But it was
his son Solomon who became
king when David died.
Solomon knew that wise
kings make good decisions.
He prayed and asked God to make him
wise so that he could understand
God's laws. God heard his prayer
and made him the wisest man who
ever lived.

Any one of us can ask God to make us wise, and He will. Let's see how Solomon's wisdom helped two women.

215

Whose Baby?

1 Kings 3:16-28

Two women brought a baby to Solomon. Each woman said the baby was hers. Solomon knew just what to do to find out who the real mother was. He said he could cut the baby in half and give one part to each woman.

But one woman pointed to the other woman and said, "No, don't hurt the baby. Give the baby to her." Then Solomon knew the woman who said this was the real mother.

Solomon wasn't really going to hurt the baby.
What was he trying to find out?

Two Kingdoms

1 Kings 12:20; 16:29–33; 17:1

After Samuel, David, and Solomon
died, God's people were split into two
kingdoms—Israel in the north and Judah
in the south. King Ahab ruled Israel.
He did many things that God said were
wrong. He worshiped idols and did more
evil than any of the kings before him.

So God sent Elijah, the prophet, to teach Ahab a lesson. Elijah told Ahab that there would be no rain for many years. This made Ahab very angry.

Ahab and his wife, Jezebel, wanted to kill Elijah. But God wanted him to live. Let's see how God protected Elijah.

Elijah Runs Away from King Ahab

1 Kings 17:7–15

Elijah had to run away from Ahab and camp near a brook. God sent birds to bring the prophet food.

When the brook dried up, God told Elijah
to go ask a certain woman for food.
"I only have enough left for one meal
for me and my son," she said. Elijah
said, "Cook for me first, and you'll be all
right." So she did.

**The woman believed what Elijah said,
and guess what? After she fed Elijah,
she never ran out of food.**

Whose God Is Real?

1 Kings 18:1, 15–24

Three years passed with no rain. Finally, God told Elijah to go meet King Ahab. "There you are, you big troublemaker," said the king. But it was really the king who had caused the trouble.

"Let's see whose god is real," Elijah said. So the king's prophets built one altar to their god, and Elijah built an altar to his God. They put offerings on each of them. Then they prayed and waited to see whose god would answer their prayers by sending fire to burn up the sacrifice.

What do you suppose Elijah was up to?

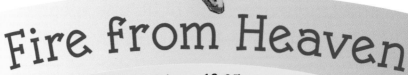

Fire from Heaven

1 Kings 18:25-46

The king's prophets screamed at their fake gods to send fire. No fire came. Elijah teased, "Pray louder." They did. But nothing happened. When they stopped, Elijah had water poured over everything on the altar he'd built. Then he prayed to God in heaven to send fire.

Fire came down. It burned up the offering, the stones, and the water. Then the people knew Elijah's God was the most powerful.

225

When Elijah prayed again, it began to rain. How do you think the king felt about that?

Elijah in the Desert

1 Kings 19:1–8

Even though rain had come, King Ahab and his evil wife, Jezebel, still wanted to kill Elijah. Elijah ran for his life to the desert. He was so tired he lay right down and went to sleep.

Soon someone tapped him on the shoulder. An angel had come to make Elijah dinner. The angel fed Elijah a second time too. Then Elijah was strong enough to make a long journey.

What do you suppose Elijah thought when an angel brought him food?

God Speaks to Elijah

1 Kings 19:9–18

Elijah was still being chased by the evil king, and that made Elijah sad. Elijah went into a cave. God said, "Stand here and I will pass by." A strong wind blew, but God didn't speak. An earthquake shook the ground, but God didn't speak.

A fire burned, but still God didn't speak. Then when it was quiet, Elijah heard the gentle voice of God. "Go find a man named Elisha. He will be a helper to you, and he will be the next prophet."

Where do you suppose Elijah found Elisha?

Elijah's Helper

1 Kings 19:19–21

Elijah left the desert right away. He found Elisha plowing a field. Elijah put his coat over the young man. That meant he wanted Elisha to be his helper. First Elisha and his family had a big feast. Then he said good-bye to his mother and father and followed Elijah.

Elijah did exactly what God told him to do. Now he and Elisha would work for God together.

A Bad Queen

1 Kings 21–22:39

King Ahab and his evil wife, Jezebel, decided they wanted a neighbor's land. Speaking badly against God or the king was against the law. Jezebel got some people to lie and say the neighbor, Naboth, had said bad things about both God and King Ahab.

So Jezebel had Naboth killed, and King Ahab took Naboth's land. Not long afterward King Ahab and his wife both died terrible deaths.

God saw what Ahab and Jezebel had done. How do you think that made God feel?

233

Chariot of Fire

2 Kings 2:1–12

Elijah was getting old. His helper, Elisha, went with him everywhere.

One day Elijah and Elisha were together when God sent a chariot and horses made of fire. The fiery horses and chariot came between Elijah and Elisha. Then *whoosh!* All of a sudden Elijah went up to heaven in a whirlwind. Elisha saw him go.

Someday we will go to heaven. It will be a wonderful place. Who do you think we'll see there?

Elijah's Coat

2 Kings 2:13–14

As the whirlwind took Elijah to heaven, his coat fell off and landed on the ground. Elisha picked it up.

236

He went to the river and hit the water with the coat. He said, "Where is the God of Elijah?" Elisha wanted to see if God's power was on him like it had been on Elijah. It was. The water split in the middle, and Elisha walked across on dry ground.

This was the first miracle God did through Elisha. Keep reading to learn about more miracles that came later.

The Miracle of the Pot of Oil

2 Kings 4:1–7

"My dead husband owed money to a man. That man is going to make my two sons his slaves," a woman told Elisha. "I have nothing but this small pot of oil."

238

"Get empty jars from your neighbors," said Elisha. "Now pour oil into them." When the woman started pouring oil from her pot, it just kept coming. She filled every jar in the house. Then she sold the oil, paid her debt to the man, and saved her boys from slavery.

How could a small pot of oil fill so many big jars and pots? It was a miracle!

Elisha Helps a Little Boy

2 Kings 4:8–37

Another woman also
begged Elisha for help.
Her little boy had
died. Elisha
went to her
house.

He went to the room where the little boy's body lay and prayed over him. The little boy sneezed and opened his eyes. He had come back to life, and he was just fine.

**This was another wonderful miracle.
Only God can give people life.**

Poison in the Stew

2 Kings 4:38–41

Elisha met some hungry men. He had
his servant make them stew. One of
the men wanted to help. He found some
plants and added them to the stew. He
didn't know they were poisonous.

When the men started eating, they cried, "There's death in the pot!" Elisha put flour into the stew, and the food became safe to eat.

243

Throwing flour into a stew doesn't usually remove poison. This was another miracle from God.

Food for Everyone

2 Kings 4:42–44

People all over Israel were running out of food. They were hungry. One man brought 20 loaves of bread to Elisha. Elisha said, "Feed the people." The man said, "We can't feed 100 men with so little bread."

Elisha told him to start feeding them and there would be bread left over. Sure enough, that's what happened!

Elisha was not doing these miracles in his own power. God was helping him. What miracle do you think happened next?

Seven Dips in the Jordan River

2 Kings 5:1–14

Naaman, an important soldier, had a terrible skin disease called *leprosy*. People who had leprosy could not come close to other people. They had to live in lepers' towns. Naaman's wife's servant girl said, "I wish my master could meet Elisha. He would heal him."

So Naaman went to find Elisha. "Wash in the Jordan River seven times, and you'll be healed," Elisha said. Naaman was embarrassed. What Elisha told him to do seemed silly. But he went to the river to wash himself, and on the seventh time the leprosy disappeared.

If a dip in the river would make you well from a terrible sickness, would you do it, even if it seemed silly?

A Floating Ax

2 Kings 6:1–7

Some men were building a meeting house for Elisha. As they were chopping down trees for the house, an ax broke. The metal part fell into the river and sank. The man who was using it yelled, "That was an ax I'd borrowed!"

Elisha threw a stick into the water, and the iron ax head floated up.

Wow! Ax heads are heavy and can't float, unless God makes them do it. God can do anything!

No Food!

2 Kings 6:24–25; 7:1–9

An army surrounded the city of Samaria, and no one could go in or come out. The people in the city had no food. God told Elisha to say that tomorrow there would be lots of food. About that time four men decided to see if the enemy would give them something to eat. When they got to the camp, there was no one there.

The soldiers had run away, leaving all their food and gold and clothes. At first the men started to hide the treasure for themselves. But then they decided to share. They told the people in the city, and soon everyone had enough to eat. It was just as Elisha said it would be.

Those four men were not selfish. They could have kept everything they found for themselves, but they didn't. What do you think God wanted them to do?

The Baby Prince

2 Kings 11:1–12:2

Joash was a baby prince. His grandmother was evil. She wanted to kill him so she could be queen. Joash's aunt hid him in God's house until he was seven years old.

Then soldiers came to God's house and got him. They made him king even though he was just a little boy. Joash ruled for 40 years in Jerusalem. He did what God said was right.

If you were made king today,
what would you do first?

The Sun Goes Backward

2 Kings 20:1–11; Isaiah 38

Hezekiah was a good king. One day he got very sick. He knew he was going to die. He prayed and asked God to let him live a little longer. Then, to be sure that God had heard him, Hezekiah asked for the sun to go backward. He asked for the shadow that was at the bottom of the steps to go back up ten steps. And just as he asked, the shadow moved back up ten steps. And Hezekiah lived 15 more years.

255

For the sun to move backward would be as amazing as falling up instead of down. It was a miracle!

Captured!

2 Kings 24:18–25:21; 2 Chronicles 36:15–23

Over and over God had warned His people not to worship idols. But they kept right on doing what God had told them not to do. So finally God let an enemy capture His people and take them from the land He'd given them. They were taken far away to a place called Babylon. It was a sad day.

God wants us to do what is right, and He is very patient. But if we continue to do wrong, we will have to suffer the consequences.

257

Beautiful Queen Esther

Esther 1–3

Years later the Persian kingdom defeated Babylon. But God's people were still living in the land of Babylon. One of them was a young woman named Esther.

The king of Persia wanted a beautiful young woman to be his queen. He picked Esther. Soon afterward one of the king's men decided to get rid of all God's people in the kingdom. Since Esther was one of them, it meant he would get rid of her too.

It must have been a very scary time for Esther. What do you think she did?

Esther Saves Her People

Esther 4–9

Esther knew it was up to her to save her people. She also knew that if she visited the king and he got angry, she wouldn't be queen anymore. The king could even have her killed. What should she do?

Esther decided to go to the king anyway. When she went, the king granted her wish that her people would be allowed to live.

Esther was very brave. She did what God wanted her to do, and because she was brave, she saved her people. Yea, Esther!

261

An Honest Man

Job 1:1–12

Job was an honest man who loved God.
He had a big family and was very rich.
Everything he did pleased God.

Then Satan, the enemy of God and man, went to God and said, "You are protecting Job from anything going wrong. That's why he obeys You." "All right," said God. "You can do anything to him except take his life."

Satan is very real. He doesn't like God, and he doesn't like us. But Job was about to find out that God is always with us.

When Bad Things Happen

Job 1:13–2:10

Awful things began to happen to Job.
His children died. His house fell down.
He got sores all over his body.

264

His cattle were taken away by robbers. His friends told him to turn away from God.

But Job never doubted that God loved him. Job was faithful to God, even in hard times.

When bad things happen, it doesn't mean God has forgotten about us. He's never far away in the bad times. And He wants us to continue to love and obey Him.

A Time for Everything

Ecclesiastes 3:1–8

There is a time for everything that happens in our lives. There are happy times and there are sad times.

266

There are times when we cry and times when we laugh.

There are times to hug and times not to hug.

There is a time to be silent and a time to speak.

A little bit of everything happens in our lives. The important thing is to stay close to God all the time.

A Message for King Ahaz

Isaiah 7:1–17; 9:2–7

God told the prophet Isaiah to take a message to a king named Ahaz. King Ahaz was in the family of King David. Isaiah told the king that someday God was going to send a child who would grow up to be a leader of all of God's people. He said that this person would be the Prince of Peace and would rule as King forever.

269

Who was Isaiah talking about? Today we know
he was talking about Jesus, God's Son.

Three Brave Men

Daniel 3:1–23

Remember how God's people were captured and taken away to the country of Babylon? The king of that country was Nebuchadnezzar. Three of these young men—Shadrach, Meshach, and Abednego—worked for King Nebuchadnezzar.

But when the king wanted them to bow down and worship a golden idol, they wouldn't do it. So the king told his soldiers to put all three men into a red-hot furnace.

God was pleased that these young men loved Him so much they would not worship the king's idol. What do you think happened next?

271

The Extra Man

Daniel 3:24–30

Guess what? The men in the furnace didn't burn up. God sent someone to protect them in the furnace. The king was surprised when he saw four people walking around. He told Shadrach, Meshach, and Abednego to come out of the furnace.

Then the king made a new law. It said that no one could say anything bad about the God of these men.

God has promised to be with us no matter what happens to us.

Writing on the Wall

Daniel 5:1–26

Daniel was one of God's people who was a slave in Babylon. One night the new king of Babylon gave a banquet. Suddenly a hand appeared and began writing on the wall something that no one could read. It was very scary!

The king asked Daniel to come and tell him what it meant. Daniel said it meant that God was angry with the king. And the kingdom of Babylon would be divided and given to two other countries, the Medes and Persians.

Daniel always lived for God no matter what anyone said. Let's see what happened to him.

Daniel Disobeys the King

Daniel 6:1–10

Daniel prayed three times every day. Some men in the new kingdom of the Medes and Persians wanted to get rid of Daniel. So they had the new king make a rule that people could only pray to the king. If someone broke the rule, he would be thrown into the lions' den.

But Daniel went to his house and got down on his knees and prayed to God just as he had always done.

Daniel knew that praying to God was more important than obeying the king's new rule.

A Den of Hungry Lions

Daniel 6:11–28

The men caught Daniel praying to God and told the king. The king was sad because he liked Daniel, but the king couldn't change the law. So Daniel was thrown into a den of hungry lions.

But wait! God sent an angel to close the mouths of the lions so they couldn't bite.

In the morning, the king came to see if God had saved Daniel, and sure enough, Daniel was just fine.

God saved Daniel. After being saved from the lions, do you think Daniel went on praying to God three times a day?

Jonah Runs Away

Jonah 1:1–3

"Go to Nineveh," God told a man named Jonah. "Tell them to stop their evil ways." Jonah got up, but he didn't go to Nineveh. He didn't like the people of that city, so he ran away.

Jonah went to the seashore. He got on
a ship going the opposite direction from
Nineveh. God saw what Jonah was doing.

**God always sees what we are doing.
He wants us to make good choices.**

A Big Storm!

Jonah 1:4-6

Jonah sailed away on the ship. When the ship was at sea, God sent a big storm. Waves pounded the ship. The sailors were very frightened of the storm.

The captain went down into the bottom of the ship and found Jonah sleeping. "Get up and pray to your God too," he said. "Maybe your God will save us!"

The captain and everyone prayed.
They knew they needed help from somebody
bigger than themselves.

Jonah Goes Overboard

Jonah 1:7–16

"Somebody has done something to cause this storm. Let's find out who it is," the sailors said. They decided the storm was Jonah's fault. "You're right. I ran away from God," Jonah told them. "Throw me into the sea. Then it will calm down."

284

So the sailors tossed Jonah overboard.
As soon as Jonah was in the water, the
sea became calm.

**You might think that would be the end of Jonah,
but it wasn't!**

Inside a Big Fish!

Jonah 1:17–2:9

Down, down into the swirling water went Jonah. Then *gulp!* Something swallowed him. Jonah was in the stomach of a big fish. God left him there to learn something important. It took three days and three nights.

Then Jonah prayed to God for help. He decided to do what God had told him to do.

It took a while for Jonah to catch on that he needed to obey God. Now, how was he going to get out of that fish?

Jonah Obeys God

Jonah 2:10–3:10

God had a plan. He spoke to that fish.
It swam up close to the beach and spit
Jonah out of its stomach onto dry land.

Right away God said to Jonah, "Get up and go to the great city of Nineveh. Say what I tell you to say." This time Jonah didn't argue. He obeyed. He jumped up and went straight to Nineveh.

**Every time we disobey, we get in trouble.
What would be a better choice?**

New Testament

An Angel's Message

Luke 1:5–20

A priest named Zachariah went to God's house to burn an incense offering. As soon as he was inside, the angel Gabriel appeared. "Zachariah, you and your wife, Elizabeth, will have a son. You will name him John," Gabriel said.

Zachariah didn't believe it was possible for Elizabeth and him to have a son. They were too old. "Because you don't believe me, Zachariah, you will not be able to talk until the baby is born," Gabriel said.

John was going to be a very important person. He would tell others to get ready because Jesus was coming.

A Baby Named John

Luke 1:57–66

Just as the angel Gabriel had said, a baby boy was born to Zachariah and his wife, Elizabeth.

294

Their friends were very happy for them. "Name him Zachariah after his father," they said. Zachariah still couldn't talk, so he wrote down, "His name is John." As soon as Zachariah wrote that, he could talk again.

His name is John.

People don't get to see angels very often, but when they do, they need to pay attention. Angels bring messages from God. What is another way God sends messages?

Mary's Big Surprise

Luke 1:26–38

Not long after his visit to Zachariah, the angel Gabriel went to see a young woman named Mary. She was a cousin to Elizabeth, Zachariah's wife. Mary lived in Nazareth and was engaged to marry Joseph, the carpenter.

296

"Don't be afraid, Mary," the angel said. "God is pleased with you. You will have a baby and will name Him Jesus. He will be called the Son of God." This was a big surprise to Mary.

What would you do if an angel suddenly appeared right here in front of you?

Joseph Marries Mary

Matthew 1:18–25

When Joseph heard the news that Mary was going to have a baby, he didn't know what to think. He wasn't married to her yet. God loved Joseph and wanted him to understand that the baby was from God and everything was going to be all right.

298

So God sent an angel to talk to Joseph in a dream. This angel told Joseph, "Name the baby Jesus. He will save people from their sins." When Joseph heard God's plan, he married Mary.

The name *Jesus* means "savior."
What does a savior do?

God's Baby Son

Luke 2:1–7

The ruler of the land, Augustus Caesar, made a new law to count all the people. Everyone had to register in their hometown. So Joseph and Mary went to their hometown, Bethlehem. The town was full of people. There was no place for Mary and Joseph to sleep.

Finally, Joseph found a place for them where the animals were kept. And that's where God's Baby Son was born. His first bed was on the hay in the box where the animals were fed.

Why do you think God would want His Son to be born where the animals were kept?

Some Sleepy Shepherds

Luke 2:8–12

That night, out in the fields, sleepy shepherds were taking care of their sheep. Suddenly an angel appeared in the sky. The angel's light was so bright, it hurt their eyes.

"Don't be afraid," the angel said. "I have good news for you. A baby was born in Bethlehem town tonight. He is your Savior. You will find Him lying in a feeding box."

Who was the first to hear about Baby Jesus?

What the Shepherds Saw

Luke 2:13–20

Then the whole sky filled up with so many angels no one could count them all. They sang, "Glory to God in heaven!" And then, when the song was over, the angels disappeared.

The shepherds hurried to Bethlehem. They found Mary and Joseph and saw Baby Jesus lying in the hay in the feeding box. The shepherds told them everything the angels had said about the child.

If you had been out there on the hill with the shepherds, what would you have been thinking when the angels left?

Gifts for Baby Jesus

Matthew 2:1–12

Soon many of the people who came to register in Bethlehem went home. Mary and Joseph moved into a house.

One day they had visitors who came from far away in the east. These visitors were wise men. They had followed a bright star to find little Jesus. They bowed down and worshiped God's only Son and gave Him expensive presents of gold, frankincense, and myrrh.

307

Why do you think the wise men came to see little Jesus?

Another Journey

Matthew 2:13–15

After the wise men left, God sent another angel to Joseph in a dream. "Take the child and Mary and go to Egypt," the angel said. "King Herod wants to kill Jesus. Stay in Egypt until I tell you it's safe to come home."

308

It was still night, but Joseph got up out of bed and took Mary and Jesus and headed for Egypt.

Joseph obeyed God immediately. And God kept his family safe. Why is it good to obey quickly?

Home at Last!

Matthew 2:19–23

Mary, Joseph, and Jesus stayed in Egypt until God sent another angel to Joseph in a dream. "Get up and take Mary and Jesus and go home," said the angel. King Herod had died. He could never hurt them again. God and His angels had kept Mary, Joseph, and Jesus safe.

So with happy hearts, they went home to live in Nazareth.

Whew! It was finally safe to go home. How do you think Mary and Joseph felt about that?

Where Is Jesus?

Luke 2:41–45

Every year Jesus' parents went to
Jerusalem to celebrate the Passover.
When Jesus was 12, they went as usual.
When Mary and Joseph started home, they
didn't see Jesus, but it was okay. They
thought Jesus was traveling with friends.

Late in the day they realized He wasn't with any of their friends. Mary and Joseph were very worried and hurried back to Jerusalem, looking for Him all along the way. They were afraid they had lost Jesus.

What are some places where Mary and Joseph might have looked for Jesus?

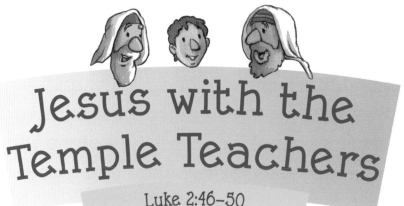

Jesus with the Temple Teachers

Luke 2:46-50

When Mary and Joseph found Jesus, He was in the Temple—a place where God's people went to worship. Twelve-year-old Jesus was talking with some teachers just like He was one of them. He asked them questions, and He answered theirs.

His mother had a question too. "Son, why did You stay behind? We were worried about You." Jesus said, "You should have known I must be where My Father's work is!"

315

The Man Who Ate Locusts

Matthew 3:1–13; Mark 1:4–9

Jesus' cousin, John, became a preacher when he grew up. He lived in the desert and wore rough clothes and ate locusts and honey. (Locusts were like grasshoppers.) John told the people to change their hearts and lives and ask forgiveness for their wrongs because Jesus was coming soon.

One day when Jesus was grown up, too, He came to the place where John was preaching and baptizing people. Jesus asked John to baptize Him in the river.

When Jesus asked John to baptize Him, do you think John did it?

John Baptizes Jesus

Matthew 3:13–17

At first John didn't want to baptize Jesus. He thought Jesus should be the one to baptize *him*. But when Jesus said it needed to be this way, John obeyed and took Jesus into the river and baptized Him.

As Jesus came up out of the water, God's Spirit, like a dove, came down to Him from heaven. God spoke and said, "This is My Son, and I love Him. I am very pleased with Him."

Jesus set a good example for us by following God's command to be baptized. Have you been baptized?

Jesus Tempted by Satan

Matthew 4:1–4

Soon God's Spirit led Jesus away from the river and into the desert. Jesus wanted to pray and think about what God wanted Him to do next. Jesus fasted—that means He didn't eat, so He got very hungry. Then the devil, Satan, appeared. Satan knew that Jesus was tired and hungry.

"Turn these rocks into bread," Satan told Jesus. Jesus knew that Satan was trying to get Him to do something wrong. Jesus had studied God's Word, so He remembered what He had learned from the Scriptures. He said, "A person does not live only by eating bread. A person lives by doing everything the Lord says."

Satan doesn't stop picking on people with just one try. He was not through with Jesus yet. Keep reading to see what happened next.

On Top of the Temple

Matthew 4:5–7

Satan took Jesus to Jerusalem and stood Him on the very top of the Temple. The Temple is where God's people worshiped. "If you are God's Son, jump down from this high place," Satan said. "It is written in the Scriptures that God's angels will catch You." That was not a smart thing for Satan to suggest, and Jesus knew it. He answered by saying, "It is also written in the Scriptures, 'Do not test God.'"

323

It is foolish to test or tease God. Testing God means doing very risky things that might get you hurt.

The Kingdoms of the World

Matthew 4:8–11

That sneaky devil, Satan, had one more test up his sleeve. He took Jesus to a high mountain and showed Him all the kingdoms of the world. Satan said, "Bow down and give honor to me, and I will give You all these things."

Jesus had an answer ready, "Go away from Me! It is written in the Scriptures, 'You must worship only the Lord God.'" So Satan went away.

Even though we can't see Satan, he tries to get us to do things that are wrong. What are some of the things Satan tries to get us to do?

Jesus Heals a Sick Boy

John 4:46–51

Jesus loved little children, and whenever He could, He helped them. One day an important man begged Jesus to come to his house and heal his sick son. But Jesus didn't go. Instead He said, "Go home. Your son will live."

326

The man believed Jesus and went home, but before he got there his servants met him and said, "Your son is well."

When we believe and trust someone to do something we cannot see, that is called *faith*. The man in this story trusted Jesus to keep a promise. Whom do you trust?

Jesus Brings a Girl Back to Life

Mark 5:22–43

Jesus also helped a little girl. Her father's name was Jairus, and he was an important man. "My little daughter is dying," Jairus said. "Please come and pray for her so she will get well and live." Before Jesus could go to the little girl, she died. But Jesus went anyway. With the child's mother and father and three of His followers, Jesus went in the girl's room and took her hand in His. "Little girl," Jesus said, "stand up!" And she did. She was well.

When we ask God for something, sometimes He says yes, and sometimes He says no. The most important thing is that He always hears us.

329

A Little Boy Helps Jesus

John 6:1–13

Great crowds of people followed Jesus to see His miracles and hear Him teach about God's love for them. The people sometimes forgot to take food with them. One day a huge crowd of 5,000 men and their families followed Jesus. It was late in the day when they reached Jesus, and the people were getting hungry.

The only one with any food was a little boy with five small loaves of bread and two fish. Jesus blessed the food. His closest followers and helpers gave it to the people. After everyone had plenty to eat, the helpers gathered up 12 baskets of leftover food.

What do you have that you could give Jesus? An offering? Some time to help someone?

Jesus Walks on the Water

Mark 6:45–53

Later that day Jesus told the followers who were His helpers to go to another city across the lake. He would come after a while. The helpers got into a boat. But that night in the middle of the lake, a strong wind came up. And the men had to work very hard to row the boat.

Then they saw something that frightened them more than the storm. They thought it was a ghost. But it wasn't a ghost. It was Jesus walking on the water. Jesus called to His helpers, "Don't be afraid." Then Jesus got into the boat, and the wind became calm.

If you had been in that boat, what would you have done?

Jesus Loves Children

Luke 18:15–17

Many people wanted to see Jesus. When Jesus saw how sick and sad they were, He wanted to help them. One day some people brought their children to Him. His helpers tried to send them away. Jesus said, "Let the little children come to Me. Don't stop them. You must love and accept God like a little child if you want to enter heaven."

334

335

If you were one of the children who got to sit on Jesus' lap, what would you say to Him?

A Very Short Man

Luke 19:1–10

Everywhere Jesus went,
there were crowds of people.
In one crowd there was a very
short man named Zacchaeus.
He wanted to see Jesus, but he
couldn't see over the crowd.
So he climbed a tree.

Jesus said, "Zacchaeus, come down so we can go to your house today." Zacchaeus hurried down and took Jesus to his home. Zacchaeus wanted to do good things. He told Jesus that he'd give half of his money to the poor.

Wouldn't it be exciting to have Jesus come to your house? What would you do if Jesus came to see you?

A Coin in a Fish

Matthew 17:24–27

Peter, one of Jesus' helpers, came to tell
Jesus it was time for Him to pay taxes.
But Jesus and Peter didn't have any
money. Jesus knew just what to do. Jesus
told Peter, "Go to the lake and catch a
fish. You will find a coin in its mouth.
Use that coin to pay our taxes."

Aren't you glad Jesus always knows the best thing to do? Talk to Him about your problems.

A Blind Man Sees Again

Mark 10:46–52

Sick people followed Jesus everywhere. They wanted Him to heal them. One man who was blind heard that Jesus was walking by. He cried out, "Jesus, please help me!" People told the man to be quiet, but Jesus asked the man, "What would you like Me to do for you?"

340

The man said, "I want to see again." So Jesus healed the man's eyes. How happy the man was to see again!

Do you know someone who is sick? You could pray right now and ask Jesus to make them well.

A Very Poor Woman

Mark 12:41–44

Jesus was watching people put their money into the collection box at the Temple where God's people worshiped. Some rich people were very proud as they put in a lot of money.

342

Then a very poor woman came. In went her two small coins. *Plunk! Plunk!* Jesus told His closest followers, "This woman gave more than the rich people with many coins. The rich people gave only what they did not need, but this poor woman gave all the money she had."

343

Why do you think the woman gave God all the money she had?

Jesus Stops a Storm

Mark 4:35–41

Jesus and His followers got into a boat and set out across the lake. Jesus was so tired that He fell asleep. Soon a strong wind began to blow. Waves came over the side of the boat. Everyone was very frightened.

They woke Jesus. "Help us, or we'll drown!" Jesus commanded the wind and waves to be still. The wind stopped, and there were no more waves coming into the boat. The lake became calm.

When you are frightened, what do you do? Remember, Jesus is always there with you. Just ask Him to help you. He will.

One Lost Sheep

Luke 15:3–7

Here is a story Jesus told. A man had 100 sheep, but he lost one. Now, what was he going to do? He left his 99 sheep safe at home and went looking for the one lost sheep.

He searched everywhere, and when he finally found the lost sheep, he was so happy. He put the sheep on his shoulders and carried it home.

How is Jesus like that shepherd looking for his one lost sheep? Remember, you are as important to Jesus as that one lost sheep was to the shepherd.

A Son Spends All His Money

Luke 15:11–13

Jesus told another story. A man had two sons. The younger son said, "Give me my share of the property and money." So the father divided the property and money between his younger son and older son.

348

The younger man went to another country far away. He had lots of fun spending every bit of his money.

Do you think the younger son was making a good decision? How do you think his father felt?

The Man Who Ate Pig Food

Luke 15:14–19

After the younger son's money was gone, he got very hungry. A man gave him a job feeding pigs. As the son fed the pigs, he was so hungry that he ate the pig food.

After a while he began to realize he had been very foolish. He said to himself, "My father's servants have plenty of food. I'm going home. I'll tell my father that I have done wrong. I'll ask him if I can just be a servant."

Wow, what a mess! What were some of the choices the son made that got him into a pigpen?

Going Home to Father

Luke 15:20–32

The younger son went home. He was worried that his father wouldn't want him. But his father had been looking for him every day for a long time.

352

When he saw his son, the father ran to meet him. He hugged him and gave him new clothes. He had a party to welcome him home. He told everyone, "My son was lost, but now he is found!"

The father in this story is like God. God sees us make bad choices, and He is sad. But He is always waiting for us to come back to Him.

Jesus' Best Friends

Luke 10:38–42

One day Jesus went to visit some best friends named Mary, Martha, and Lazarus. Martha was busy getting the meal ready. Mary was sitting and listening to Jesus talk.

Martha became angry and complained, "Jesus, don't You care that Mary left me to do all this work alone? Tell her to help me." Jesus said, "What Mary is learning from Me can never be taken away from her."

Why was Martha angry? What did Jesus tell her?

Jesus Brings Lazarus Back to Life

John 11:1–44

One day Lazarus got very sick. Mary and Martha sent a message to Jesus asking Him to come heal their brother. Even though Jesus loved His three friends, He waited two days to start the trip to see them, and Lazarus died before Jesus got there.

Martha and Mary said, "If You had come earlier, our brother wouldn't have died." Jesus was so sad He cried. Then He went to the tomb of Lazarus. He said, "Lazarus, come out!" And out came Lazarus, wrapped in the burial cloths. He was alive and well!

Sometimes when we ask Jesus for something, we have to wait—sometimes for a long time.

One Man Says Thank You

Luke 17:11–19

Ten men met Jesus as He was walking along a road. They didn't come close to Jesus because they had the horrible skin disease, leprosy. They called out, "Please help us!" Jesus told them they were healed and sent them on their way.

358

As the men went on their way, the leprosy disappeared. Only one man came back. He bowed down to Jesus and thanked Him for what He had done.

We should remember to say thank you for what God has done for us. What has God done for you?

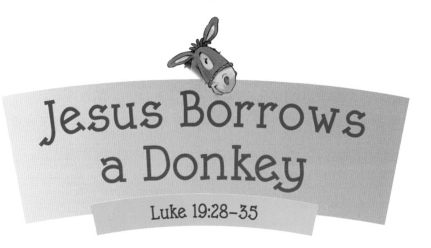

Jesus Borrows a Donkey

Luke 19:28–35

The first Passover happened when God's people left Egypt long ago. After that, God's people celebrated the Passover every year. One year Jesus and His closest followers went to Jerusalem to celebrate the Passover.

Before they got there, Jesus said to
His followers, "Go into town and find a
young donkey colt. Untie it and bring
it to Me. If anyone asks where you are
taking it, say, 'The Master needs it.'"
When the men got back with the donkey
colt, they spread their coats on
its back. Jesus climbed
on the colt.

Why do you suppose Jesus needed that donkey colt?

Jesus Rides Like a King

Luke 19:36–38; John 12:12–16

The donkey started to clippity-clop through the town. People came running. They threw their coats down for the donkey to walk on. They took palm branches and waved them in the air. "Praise God!" they shouted.

362

Some of them remembered the Scriptures that said, "Your king is coming . . . sitting on the colt of a donkey."

Why do you suppose they laid their coats down for the donkey to walk on?
Did they think Jesus was a king?

Jesus Shows How to Serve

John 13:1–17

Soon it was time for the Passover dinner. Jesus and His closest followers gathered in a big room. Jesus stood up, took off His coat, got some water in a wash bowl, and wrapped a towel around His waist.

Then He started washing His followers' feet. Jesus did this to teach His friends they were to serve one another.

Jesus was serving His followers to set a good example. What could you do to serve your brothers and sisters and parents?

The First Lord's Supper

Matthew 26:26–29; 1 Corinthians 11:23–25

While Jesus and His closest followers were eating the Passover dinner, Jesus took some bread and thanked God for it. He broke the bread apart and said, "Take this bread and eat it. Do this to remember Me."

Next He took a cup and said, "When you drink this juice of the grape, remember Me." Jesus knew this was His last meal with His followers because He was about to be killed. He wanted His followers to always remember Him.

Today in church we still eat bread and drink the juice of the grape to remember Jesus. We call this time of remembering *Communion* or *The Lord's Supper*.

Jesus Prays for Help

Matthew 26:36–40; Mark 14:32–42; Luke 22:39–46

Jesus and His followers went straight from dinner to a quiet garden. Jesus wanted to pray and ask God to make Him strong for what was about to happen. He took three of His closest followers—Peter, James, and John—with him. Jesus asked them to wait and pray.

He went a little farther into the garden so that He could pray by Himself. It was very late, and the three men were very tired. They couldn't keep their eyes open to pray. Soon they were asleep. Jesus woke them twice, but they went back to sleep each time.

When we have tough things ahead of us, we need to pray and ask God to help us.

Jesus Is Arrested

Matthew 26:45–56; Luke 22:45–51;
John 18:10–11

The third time Jesus woke His followers, He said, "We must go. Here comes the man who has turned against Me." Just then a big crowd carrying torches and clubs came into the garden. Judas, one of Jesus' followers, was with them. He kissed Jesus on the cheek. It was a signal to the guards to arrest Jesus.

Peter pulled out his sword and cut off the ear of one guard. Jesus told Peter to put the sword away. Then He healed the guard's ear.

You might think the crowd would let Jesus go after He healed the man's ear. Well, they didn't They arrested Him and took Him away.

Pilate Questions Jesus

Luke 22:52–23:25

Lots of people loved Jesus, but there were many who didn't like Him at all. After Jesus was captured in the garden, He was taken to the house of the high priest, then to Pilate, the Roman governor of Judea.

All night the rulers asked Jesus if He was God's Son. They did not believe that He was. Finally Pilate said that he didn't think Jesus was guilty. But the people who hated Jesus kept yelling until Pilate decided that Jesus had to die on a cross.

Jesus told everyone that He was God's Son, and that made some people very angry. But even if they didn't believe it, He was still God's Son.

Jesus Is Killed on a Cross

Matthew 27:27–40; Mark 15:25–27

Pilate's soldiers took Jesus and put a crown of thorns on His head and made fun of Him. Then they led Jesus out of the city to a place called Golgotha to be killed on a cross.

At nine o'clock in the morning, the soldiers nailed Jesus to the cross. They also put two robbers beside Jesus, one on the right and one on the left.

The day God's Son died on the cross was a sad day. But God had a wonderful plan. Keep reading and you'll see what it was.

A Dark Day

Matthew 27:45–54; Luke 23:44–49;
Hebrews 9

While Jesus was on the cross, the land
became dark from noon until three
o'clock. Then Jesus died, and there was a
big earthquake.

When the earth shook, the thick curtain in the Temple between the Holy Place and the Most Holy Place ripped from top to bottom. Now people could see inside the Most Holy Place. Before, only the High Priest got to see inside. When the soldiers at the cross saw what happened when Jesus died, they knew He really was the Son of God!

Jesus died because He loved us. He died so that our sins could be forgiven. Let's tell Him right now that we love Him for what He did on the cross.

Jesus Is Laid in a Tomb

Luke 23:50–56

A rich man, named Joseph of Arimathea, had a new tomb where he had planned to be buried. He took Jesus' body from the cross and put it in his own empty tomb.

Joseph and Jesus' friends wrapped His body in strips of linen and laid it carefully in the tomb. Roman soldiers came to guard the tomb. They rolled a huge stone over the door and sealed it in a way that would show if anyone tried to move the stone.

Everyone thought that since Jesus was dead, they would never see Him again. They were in for a big surprise!

A Big Surprise

Matthew 28:1–10

The day after Jesus was buried was a holy day, so His friends had to stay home. Then very early on Sunday morning, the first day of the week, the women went back to the tomb. It was the third day since Jesus died.

When the women got there, they couldn't believe their eyes. The stone had been rolled away! An angel of God was sitting on the stone! The soldiers were so frightened they were like dead men.

How do you think those women at the tomb felt when they saw the angel?

Jesus Is Alive!

Matthew 28:5–8; Luke 24:9–12

The angel said, "Don't be afraid. Jesus is alive." Those women were as happy as they could be! They ran to find other friends of Jesus.

Some of Jesus' friends didn't believe what the women said. But everything the women said was true. Jesus was alive! He had risen from death.

How long is forever? Jesus promised He would come back to life . . . and He did. Jesus is alive today and will be forever.

Jesus Eats Dinner with Two Friends

Luke 24:13–32

Two of Jesus' friends were walking along the road, and Jesus joined them. These two people didn't know it was Jesus who was walking with them. But they liked talking with this man.

384

They invited Him to have dinner at their house. Jesus came, and while He was thanking God for the food, the friends realized the man was Jesus. Then Jesus disappeared.

After Jesus was raised from the dead, He could appear and disappear. What would you do if Jesus suddenly appeared here?

Jesus Appears to a Room Full of Friends

Luke 24:33–49

One night Jesus appeared in a room where many of His friends were gathered. He told them to tell their family and friends and neighbors and even strangers that He is alive.

386

He told them to share everything He had
taught them. They were to tell the people
in Jerusalem first, but then they were to
tell people everywhere. Jesus told them
to wait in Jerusalem until God sent them
a special gift of power from heaven.

**Whom do you know that would like
to hear all about Jesus' love?**

Jesus Goes to Heaven

Luke 24:50–53; Acts 1:6–11

Jesus led His followers a little way out of town. Jesus prayed for His followers, and while He was praying, He started to rise up into heaven. Then a cloud hid Him from His followers.

388

As everyone was standing there staring up into heaven, two angels appeared beside them and said, "Jesus has been taken away from you and into heaven. He will come back in the clouds, just like He went away."

Remember the gift that God was going to send?
Keep reading and see what happened.

God's Spirit Comes to Help

Acts 2:1–4

After Jesus went back to heaven, His friends and helpers were praying together in a big room. Suddenly something amazing happened.

First it sounded as if a huge wind were blowing. Next flames of fire flickered over every person's head. Then God's Spirit came, and everyone began to speak in different languages. This was the gift from God that Jesus had promised His followers.

Jesus' friends were happy. God's Spirit had come to live with them and to help them.

Everyone Hears and Understands

Acts 2:5–42

The night that God's Spirit came to Jesus' followers, there were people from many countries in Jerusalem. These people spoke different languages.

When they heard Jesus' friends praying, they went to see what the noise was all about. They found Jesus' friends telling about the great things God had done.

But they were all surprised to hear it in their own language. "What does this mean?" they asked.

God's Holy Spirit still helps those who follow Jesus today.

A Beggar at the Temple

Acts 2:43–3:10

After that day when the Holy Spirit first came, Jesus' followers began to do many miracles, telling people about God's love and how Jesus had come to save them. One afternoon Peter and John went to the Temple. A man who couldn't walk sat there begging for money. Peter looked at him and said, "I don't have any money, but I do have something else I can give you: By the power of Jesus Christ from Nazareth— stand up and walk!" Up jumped the man. His feet and ankles were now strong.

Do you know someone who is sick? Now is a good time to pray and ask Jesus to help them.

Philip Meets an Ethiopian

Acts 8:26–31

Philip was another one of Jesus' followers. He was busy telling people about Jesus when an angel spoke to him. "Go out on the road," the angel said. Along came a very important man from Ethiopia riding in his chariot. He was reading from the book of Isaiah.

Philip ran alongside the chariot and said, "Do you understand what you are reading?" No, the man didn't understand. He stopped the chariot and invited Philip to ride in the chariot and explain what the book meant.

God looks for people, like Philip, who are ready to do what He asks.

Philip Baptizes the Ethiopian

Acts 8:32–40

Philip explained the Scripture passage the man was reading. It was all about Jesus. The man asked, "Why don't I get baptized?" The Ethiopian man believed in Jesus, and he wanted to be baptized.

So they stopped the chariot, and Philip baptized him. Then God needed Philip in another place, and *whoosh!* Just like that, Philip was gone.

When we do what God asks of us, we don't know what will happen next. We just need to be ready for whatever it is.

A Mean Man

Acts 9:1–4

There was a mean man chasing after Jesus' followers. His name was Saul. He was sure that everything he heard about Jesus was wrong. He didn't believe any of it. He was sure he was right. So he hurt, and even killed, people who believed in Jesus.

Well, God wanted Saul to work for Him. So one day when Saul was on a journey, God sent a bright flash of light. It was so bright, Saul fell to the ground.

Why do you think God wanted Saul to work for Him?

Saul Is Blinded

Acts 9:4–9

"Saul! Why are you doing things against Me?" a voice said from inside the light. "Who are you?" asked Saul. "I am Jesus. Now get up and go into the city."

When Saul stood up, he was blind. His friends had to lead him into the city. Saul wouldn't eat or drink anything for three days.

What will happen to poor, blind Saul?
Do you think he is ready to listen to God?

Ananias
Helps Saul

Acts 9:10–18; 13:9

God sent a man named Ananias to find
Saul and pray for him so that Saul could
see again. Ananias was scared of Saul.
But Ananias believed in Jesus and went
anyway.

Ananias prayed for Saul, and Saul's sight came back. On that day, God changed Saul's heart to make him kind to those who believed in Jesus. Saul was also called Paul. Soon Paul began to tell others about Jesus too.

Did you know that Paul became one of the greatest preachers who ever lived?

Peter in Jail

Acts 12:1–18

One day mean King Herod threw Peter, one of Jesus' followers, in jail. The king had 16 soldiers guard Peter so he couldn't get away. That night an angel came into Peter's cell. "Hurry! Get up!" the angel said. "Follow me." Peter thought he must be dreaming . . . but he wasn't. The chains fell off his hands, and the angel led him past the guards. When they came to the iron gate of the prison, it swung open on its own, and Peter was free.

God is always stronger than anything that can happen to us. We have to trust that He will always do what's best for us.

A Woman Who Sold Purple Cloth

Acts 16:12–15

After Paul became a follower of Jesus, he went everywhere teaching people about Jesus. Many times there was no building where he could meet with friends. One day he and his friends were looking for a place to meet by the river when they saw a group of women.

One woman was Lydia. Her job was selling purple cloth. She loved God, but didn't know about Jesus. Paul told her all about Jesus, and Lydia believed that Jesus was God's Son. Lydia invited Paul and his friends to stay at her house.

Some of your friends probably want to know Jesus. They are just waiting for someone to tell them about Him. You could be the one who tells them.

Earthquake!

Acts 16:16–36

Some people didn't like what
Paul was preaching about
Jesus. So they
caught Paul
and his helper,
Silas, and threw
them in jail. The two
men were beaten, and
their feet were fastened
tightly so they couldn't
run away. That night,
instead of complaining
or crying, Paul and Silas
prayed and sang songs
to God.

Suddenly there was an earthquake, and the jail doors popped open. The jailer thought his prisoners had escaped. He knew if the prisoners had escaped, he would be in big trouble. Paul called to him, "We are all here!" When the jailer came to them, he asked, "What must I do to be saved?" Paul told him all about Jesus.

If you had been beaten, thrown in jail, and had your feet pinned down, what would you be doing?

Some People Laugh at Paul

Acts 17:16–34

Paul traveled to Athens in Greece to tell
people about Jesus. In Athens, Paul saw
an altar with writing that said, "TO A
GOD WHO IS NOT KNOWN." Paul began to
preach. He told the people about the God
who made the whole world.

Paul said that God doesn't live in temples that men build, but in their hearts. He told them about Jesus coming back to life after being dead. Some of the people laughed at Paul, but some of the people believed in Jesus.

TO A GOD WHO IS NOT KNOWN.

God wants all of us to tell others the Good News that Jesus is alive. Some people will believe, and some will laugh. We must pray for all of them.

413

Shipwrecked!

Acts 27

Paul got on a big ship. He was going to the city of Rome. The ship went very slowly because of strong winds blowing against it. Finally, the ship came to a safe harbor, and Paul told the captain he didn't think it was a good idea to leave the harbor for a while. But the captain disagreed, and he sailed anyway.

Soon a wind came up and blew hard on the ship. The sailors couldn't steer it. Paul knew they were in trouble—they might sink. He told the sailors to eat so they would be strong for the trouble ahead. Before long, the ship hit a sandbank and began to break into pieces. Everyone had to jump into the sea and swim for the beach. They all made it to shore safely.

How scary! A shipwreck! Where did they land? What happened next?

A Poisonous Snake

Acts 28:1–6

All the people from the shipwreck were now on the island of Malta, near the country of Greece. The people who lived on the island were very kind. They built a fire and invited the passengers to warm themselves.

Paul helped by gathering wood for the fire, and as he did, a poisonous snake bit him on the hand. Paul just shook the snake off into the fire. He was not even hurt. The island people waited for him to fall down dead from the poison, but Paul was just fine.

Why do you think Paul did not die when the poisonous snake bit him?

New Heaven and Earth

Revelation 21

One of the biggest promises God ever made was that we will live with Him in heaven forever. He said that there would be a new heaven and a new earth and we would get a new body—one that won't get old but will live forever.

In the new heaven, no one will ever be sad again. No one will ever die again. The streets will be made of gold, and there will be gates of pearl. Everything will be more beautiful than anything you can imagine. And best of all, Jesus will be there. We will be with Him forever.

What is the most beautiful thing you have ever seen? Heaven will be a thousand times more beautiful.

Dear Parents

Spending quality time together with your family is easy and fun with this book of 52 Bible-inspired topics. You'll be creating memories while helping your children develop the life skills they need as they discover how events in the Bible really do relate to their lives today.

In each devotional I've included a variety of age-appropriate topic introductions (ranging from songs and poems to recipes and stories), a Bible verse (short enough for a child to memorize), a Bible story, "Let's Talk about It" questions, a "Share God's Love" activity, and a prayer.

My prayer is that you and your family will begin a tradition of time together that will bring joy into your lives long past the conclusion of this book.

 Blessings,
Gwen Ellis

Tips on How to Use This Devotional

- Choose one topic a week to read and discuss with your children or class. The more you create fun and lively discussions, the more your children will respond, listen, and look forward to your next time together.

- Read the short stories, poems, songs, and Bible stories in an entertaining way. Then encourage your children to act out the scene using different voices for different characters.

- Involve older children as readers.

- Encourage children to talk about the topic during mealtime, drive time, and at other times throughout the week.

- Have each child think of ways that the topic relates to his or her life, and then encourage the child to apply it.

- Do the activity (which may include playing games, creating crafts, baking, or discussing the topic) sometime during the week.

God Made Them All

Through his power all things were made—things in heaven and on earth, things seen and unseen. —COLOSSIANS 1:16

Did you know God made everything? He made all the beautiful and wonderful things we see: birds, fish, elephants, puppies, kittens, flowers, you, and me—everything! God made it all. How wonderful and awesome God is! Together let's celebrate what He has made by saying or singing the poem below.

ALL THINGS
BRIGHT AND BEAUTIFUL

All things bright and beautiful,
All creatures great and small,
All things wise and wonderful,
The Lord God made them all.
—Cecil Alexander (excerpt)

Genesis 1–2

In the beginning God made heaven and earth. Then God said, "Let there be light. Let there be plants. Let there be living things in the oceans. Let there be birds in the sky. Let there be animals on earth." And every time God said, "Let there be . . ." it happened!

Then God made people. First He made Adam. Later He made Eve so Adam would not be alone. God made both Adam and Eve like Himself. And God said it was all "Good"!

Read and Share Together

Let's Talk about It!
★ What are some other things God made?
★ Who did God make to be like Himself?
★ What did God say about everything He had made?

Share God's Love
A fun way to celebrate all the bright and beautiful things God made is to make a creation collage of pictures. Ask a grownup to help you with this activity. Find some magazines that everyone has finished reading, a large piece of paper, and a pencil, pen, or crayon. At the top of your paper write: God Made Them All. Next, tear out or cut out pictures of things God has made. Glue as many of these pictures as you can onto the paper. Hang your paper with all the pictures in your room and thank God every day for all the things He has made. When friends see the collage of pictures on your wall, share God's love by telling them how God created the world.

Prayer
Dear Lord, thank You for making our beautiful world and all the animals, birds, and fish. Thank You for making everyone I love and for making me too. Amen.

Patient Noah

We show that we are servants of God by living a pure life,
by our understanding, by our patience, and by our kindness.
—2 CORINTHIANS 6:6

A patient person waits calmly and without complaining. How patient
are you? Is it hard for you to wait your turn when playing a game or to
wait to eat just-baked cookies? What about waiting for your birthday
or to open Christmas gifts?

Here's a fun way to find out how patient you really are. (To
make it even more fun, include other family members.)
Set a timer for one minute. Then sit perfectly still,
not moving a muscle except to breathe. Did it
seem as if one minute would never pass? Set the
timer again, and this time while you are waiting
have someone tell a story. Did the time go faster
when you were busy? Staying busy and doing
something useful while being
patient is a good plan.

In today's Bible story,
see how patiently
Noah waited in the
big boat with all
those smelly
animals.

427

Bible Story

Genesis 7:12; 8:1–19

You may know the story of Noah and how God saved Noah and his family from a big flood. Noah obeyed God and built a big boat, sometimes called Noah's Ark, and filled it with animals just as God told him to do. But did you know that they were in the boat for more than a year? That is a long time to be in a floating zoo! Everyone and every creature on that ark practiced patience as they waited for the day to come when they could leave the boat.

One day Noah went to the top of the boat and opened the window he had made. He sent a dove out to see if it could find dry land. If it did, they could get off the boat. The bird came back because it couldn't find a dry place to land. Noah waited seven days and sent the dove out again. This time it came back with a green leaf in its mouth. He waited seven more days and sent the bird out again, and this time it did not come back. Noah knew that meant the dove had found a safe home, because the water on the ground was drying up. Soon Noah and his family could get off the boat. Their waiting would be over.

Read and Share Together

Let's Talk about It!

* How long were Noah, his family, and the animals on the ark?
* What did everyone on that boat have to practice?
* How many times did Noah send the dove out to find land?

Share God's Love

Yikes! Just think what it would be like to not go outside for a whole year. Being patient isn't easy, but it is something God wants us to do. There are lots of different ways to keep busy while you're being patient.

❖ On a car trip try acting out different animals sleeping or seeing how many cars you can count in your favorite color.
❖ At home you might read a book or play a game.

What are other things you can do while you're being patient?

Prayer

*Dear Lord, please help me to be patient in everything I do.
And thank You for being patient with me. Amen.*

430

Being Cheerful and Kind

Do not forget to do good to others. And share with them what you have. These are the sacrifices that please God. —HEBREWS 13:16

Are you always cheerful and kind? Are you helpful to others? Or do you complain when someone asks for your help? In the picture on this page Abby and Casey are raking the leaves in their neighbor's yard. What are some of the things you can do to be kind and helpful?

In today's Bible story, let's read together about a kind girl named Rebekah.

K is for the **King** of kings you see,
I is for **Inside**, where He lives with me,
N is for **Not**, for I will **Not** fail the King,
D is for **Devotion**—His praises I will sing.

Bible Story

Genesis 24:15–20

Abraham's servant had traveled a long time. He was thirsty and so were his ten camels. Finally, he saw a water well. Near the well was a girl named Rebekah. He asked her, "Will you give me some water, please?"

"Yes," Rebekah answered. Then she cheerfully gave the servant some water. "I will give all your camels water too," she said.

Rebekah poured water . . . and poured water . . . and still the camels were thirsty! But Rebekah did not get grumpy or complain; with a happy heart she kept getting water from the well until the camels were no longer thirsty.

Read and Share Together

Let's Talk about It!
★ What did Abraham's servant ask Rebekah?
★ What was her answer?
★ What else did Rebekah do?

Share God's Love
That was a lot of camels to give water! Did you know that when you are kind to others and help with a cheerful heart as Rebekah did, you are sharing God's love? Putting away your toys and other things without being told is a way you can be helpful.

See how many toys you can put away
in five minutes.

Ready, set, **GO!**

Prayer
*Dear God, help me to be a cheerful helper
and show kindness to others. Amen.*

The Angry Brother

When you are angry, do not sin. And do not go on being angry all day. —EPHESIANS 4:26

Have you ever been angry with a brother or sister or friend? Esau was angry with his brother, Jacob. Their argument started when Esau realized he had traded his share of their father's property (his birthright) for a bowl of soup. Let's use our time together to make a soup like Jacob's soup. Ask whoever prepares the meals in your family to help you.

JACOB'S SOUP

1 cup dry lentils
1 onion, chopped
3 stalks of celery, diced (optional)
3 carrots, grated
1 pinch of cinnamon

¼ teaspoon of ginger
½ teaspoon of cloves
1 teaspoon cummin (optional)
6 cups of water or broth (chicken, beef, or vegetable)

Pick through the dry lentils to make sure there are no stones or dirt. Rinse and put them in a pot. Put everything else in the same pot and bring it to a boil. Reduce heat and simmer for 1½ hours. Serve with pita bread.

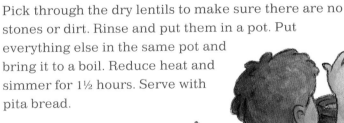

Hint: You can also ask a grownup to buy lentil soup in a can and help you prepare it.

435

Genesis 25:27–34; 27:1–37, 43–44

Esau and Jacob were brothers. Esau was the oldest, which meant when their father's property was divided, Esau would get the most. It was called his "birthright."

One day Jacob made soup while his brother, Esau, went hunting. When Esau came home, he was very, very hungry. "Let me eat some of that soup," Esau said.

"I'll trade you some soup for your birthright," Jacob answered.

Foolishly, Esau agreed to the trade. Their father gave Esau's birthright to Jacob.

Later, Esau thought, *That trade was a big mistake. My birthright is worth more than a bowl of soup!* Esau became very angry. His anger made Jacob afraid. Jacob went far away to his uncle's house, and Jacob did not come home for a long time.

Let's Talk about It!

★ What did Jacob cook?

★ Why did Esau get angry with Jacob?

Share God's Love

It's okay to be angry, but don't let your anger lead you to do something you know is wrong. Animals get angry in a different way than people—especially people who love Jesus. Try this pretend game to show the difference:

✤ Act like a big, angry bear.

✤ Act like a mad tiger.

✤ Act like an angry monkey.

✤ Now, act like a person who loves Jesus even when you are angry by being kind and thoughtful.

Prayer

Dear Lord, when I am angry, help me to remember to calm down and think about what I'm doing and saying. Amen.

A Happy Heart

A happy heart is like good medicine. —PROVERBS 17:22

Have you ever been unhappy and whined when things didn't go your way? Did whining help? Probably not. God knows things won't always go the way we want them to, but He wants us to be happy and joyful because of all He has done for us by sending Jesus as our Savior. Jesus lives in our hearts and brings joy to us. The next time you're tempted to whine about something, sing a song of joy. You can even make up a new song.

439

Exodus 4:29–5:9; 14:29–15:16

When the Israelites heard that God had sent Moses to help them get their freedom from the king of Egypt, they were happy and thanked God for remembering them. But then things didn't go as they expected!

The king would not give them their freedom. Instead, the king made them work harder!

Now they even had to find their own straw to make bricks.

That must have made the Israelites grumpy and unhappy with God and Moses. The Israelites didn't understand that this was all part of God's plan to free them. Later, when God helped the Israelites across the Red Sea to freedom, they were so happy they sang a song to praise God.

Read and Share Together

Let's Talk about It!

★ What made the Israelites unhappy?

★ What did they not understand?

★ What did the Israelites do when they were happy?

Share God's Love

When we are grumpy like the Israelites were when things go wrong in our lives, we squish joy from our hearts. Here's a fun way to see how joyful your heart is.

> Get a jar and a handful of beans. Every time you whine or pout or complain, put a bean in the jar. At the end of the week, count your beans and see how you are doing. One bean means you did well. But if you have a lot of beans, you have squished too much joy from your heart and need to work on smiling more and whining less.

Prayer

Dear Lord, I don't want to be a whiner. Help me be happy and cheerful with a heart full of joy. Amen.

God Can Do Anything

"God can do everything!" —LUKE 1:37

God takes care of you every place you go—school, camping, the seashore, visiting friends, home. He takes care of all His people all the time, everywhere. God can do anything! He used a miracle to take care of the Israelites when they left Egypt. Read today's Bible story to see just what an amazing thing God did for them. Moses was so happy, he sang the words below in praise to God. Let's sing them together.

THE SONG OF MOSES

"Are there any gods like you, Lord?
No! There are no gods like you.
You are wonderfully holy.
You are amazingly powerful.
You do great miracles."
—Exodus 15:11 (excerpt)

Bible Story

Exodus 14:5–31

Moses led God's people out of Egypt and right to the banks of a huge sea. There was no way to cross to the other side of the sea. And to make matters worse, the king of Egypt had changed his mind and sent his army to capture them. God's people thought they were trapped. But God was with them. God moved a tall cloud behind them to hide them from the Egyptians. He told Moses to raise his hand over the sea.

444

God sent a wind that pushed the seawater apart and made a path right through the middle. And guess what? That path was dry. The people didn't even get their sandals muddy as they walked safely across to the other side. Only God can do a miracle like that!

And did you know that when the Egyptian army tried to use the path, the water came back together! And that was the end of the king's army.

Read and Share Together

Let's Talk about It!
★ Where did Moses lead God's people?
★ Who was coming behind them?
★ What did God do?

Share God's Love
God takes care of everyone and everything. And He can do anything, like part the Red Sea. Find out just how awesome this miracle was by making a small sea.

A SMALL SEA

Start by filling a small bowl halfway with sand or dirt. Go to the sink and add enough water to cover the sand with about an inch of water over the top. With your hands, try to separate the water into two parts. You can't do it, can you? Now pour the water off the sand. Feel the sand. How long do you think it would take for the sand to get dry?

Prayer
Dear Lord, You helped Your people cross the Red Sea. I know You can take care of me too. Thank You for loving me. Amen.

446

God Takes Care of Us

My God will use his wonderful riches in Christ Jesus
to give you everything you need. —PHILIPPIANS 4:19

Has your parent or teacher ever asked you to clean up a spill, but then
didn't give you any towels to do the job? Probably not. When God asks
us to do something, He gives us everything we need to do it. When
Moses led God's people out of Egypt and into the desert, there was no
water and no food. God provided them a miracle food called "manna."

AMAZING FOOD

No one knows for sure what manna was, but the Bible tells us this:
- Manna came on the ground at night and looked like frost.
- Manna looked like small white seeds.
- Manna tasted like wafers made with honey.

447

Exodus 15:22–17:7

After God's people left Egypt, they began to grumble. "In Egypt we had all the food we wanted," they complained. "Now we will starve in the desert!" God heard them and said He would be sure they had plenty of food. In the evening, He would provide them meat to eat. In the morning, He would give them all the bread they wanted. And He did.

The bread was like nothing God's people had seen before. Thin flakes came on the ground like frost, and the people had to gather it every morning. They didn't know what it was, so they called it manna, which means, "What is it?" Now they had food to eat while they lived in the desert.

Read and Share Together

Let's Talk about It!
★ What did the people want?
★ How did they act?
★ What did God send to feed them?

Share God's Love
We don't know what manna was, but we know it was sweet and white. The cookie recipe below might taste a little like manna. Ask a grownup to help you make these cookies. Then share them with others as you tell the story of God's manna miracle.

MANNA COOKIES

½ cup butter   2 teaspoons honey
1 cup sugar   ½ teaspoon vanilla
2 eggs   2 cups flour

Cream butter and sugar; add eggs and mix well. Add honey and vanilla. Slowly mix in the flour. Place half teaspoon of dough for each cookie on a baking sheet. Bake at 400 degrees for 8 minutes or until done. Makes three dozen cookies.

Prayer
Dear Lord, I trust You to take care of me.
Thank You for all You do for me. Amen.

450

God's Book

Your word is like a lamp for my feet and a light for my way.
—PSALM 119:105

Did you know that the most important book in the world is the Bible? The Bible is God's Word. It tells us everything we need to know about God, His Son Jesus, and how to live happy lives. The Bible is divided into the Old Testament and the New Testament. It's actually made up of 66 small books—39 Old Testament books and 27 New Testament books. If you know a song that names the books of the Bible, practice singing it now.

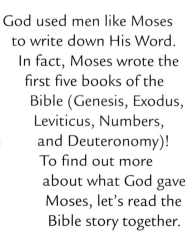

God used men like Moses to write down His Word. In fact, Moses wrote the first five books of the Bible (Genesis, Exodus, Leviticus, Numbers, and Deuteronomy)! To find out more about what God gave Moses, let's read the Bible story together.

451

Exodus 20:2–17; 24:12–18; 31:18

One day God called Moses to the top of a mountain to talk. That's when God gave Moses the Ten Commandments—ten rules—so that God's people would know how He wanted them to live. God wrote the rules on stone with His own finger.

THE TEN COMMANDMENTS

1. God is the only true God. Love and worship only Him.
2. Do not worship or serve any other god or idol.
3. Do not use God's name thoughtlessly.
4. Keep the Sabbath day holy.
5. Honor your father and your mother.
6. Do not murder anyone.
7. Husbands and wives must be faithful to each other.
8. Do not steal.
9. Do not tell lies.
10. Do not wish for someone else's things.

453

Read and Share Together

Let's Talk about It!

★ What did God use to write the Ten Commandments on stone?

★ Why did God give His people rules?

★ Who wrote the first five books of the Bible?

Share God's Love

Isn't it great to know that God loved us so much that He gave us the Bible to help us live happy lives! One way to share God's love is to tell someone why the Bible is the most important book in the world.

For fun, practice saying the first five books of the Bible.

Ready, set, **GO!**

Genesis Exodus Leviticus Numbers Deuteronomy

Prayer

Dear Lord, thank You for the Bible.
Help me to always live by Your rules. Amen.

Try Something New

"The Lord your God will be with you everywhere you go."
—JOSHUA 1:9

Have you ever surprised yourself by being able to do something you didn't think you could do? Perhaps at first it was a little scary, like the first time you tried to ride a bike. Maybe you felt like the little engine who was asked to do a big job. Do you know that story?

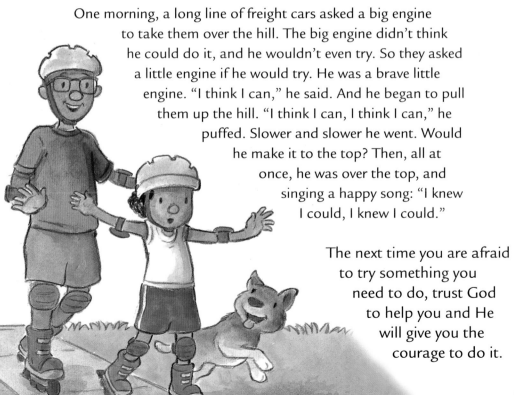

One morning, a long line of freight cars asked a big engine to take them over the hill. The big engine didn't think he could do it, and he wouldn't even try. So they asked a little engine if he would try. He was a brave little engine. "I think I can," he said. And he began to pull them up the hill. "I think I can, I think I can," he puffed. Slower and slower he went. Would he make it to the top? Then, all at once, he was over the top, and singing a happy song: "I knew I could, I knew I could."

The next time you are afraid to try something you need to do, trust God to help you and He will give you the courage to do it.

455

Numbers 13:1–14:35

One day Moses sent 12 men to explore the land God was going to give His people. The land had lots of good food, but it also had large walls and people who were like giants. When the 12 men came back, 10 of them said, "We can't go in and take over the land." They were afraid to trust God and try something new. Two men, Joshua and Caleb, said, "Don't worry. God is with us, and He is stronger than any giants." But the people were still afraid to go into the new land. Because the people didn't trust God to help them, they had to wander in the desert for 40 years.

Read and Share Together

Let's Talk about It!
* ★ How many of the men who came back wanted to try something new?
* ★ What did the others say?
* ★ What happened because the people did not believe God could help them enter the land He wanted to give them?

Share God's Love
Are you like Joshua and Caleb and trust God to help you do what He needs you to do? Name some things you have had to be brave to try. Here are some ideas to get you thinking:

* ✤ Going to your first day of school
* ✤ Learning to swim
* ✤ Trying new foods

Prayer
*Dear Lord, help me to be courageous and remember
You are always with me. Amen.*

Blind Trust

Happy is the person who trusts the Lord. —PSALM 34:8

Who do you trust? When we trust someone, it means we *believe* that person will do what's best for us—even if we don't always understand how it will happen. When Maddie trusted her mother, she got a fun surprise.

Maddie didn't understand why her mother wanted her to clean her room right then. But she stopped playing and did what her mother asked. Soon she was glad she had, because her mother had a big surprise for her. Maddie's best friend was coming over to swim and spend the night.

And Maddie was all ready to play because she had done what she'd been asked even when she didn't understand why. She had trusted her mother.

In today's Bible story, we see how God gave the Israelites some instructions that didn't seem to make much sense. But when they trusted God and did what He said, an amazing thing happened.

459

Joshua 6

God wanted His people to capture the city of Jericho. Now Jericho was a city surrounded by huge walls. The people of Jericho closed the big heavy gates in the wall and guarded them so no one could go in or out of the city.

Joshua was the leader of God's people. God told Joshua to tell the people to march around the city of Jericho once a day for six days. The priests were to march in front of the Holy Box with some soldiers in front of them and other soldiers behind the Holy Box.

Then on the seventh day, He wanted them to march around the city seven times. And that's not all. God said the priests were to blow their horns and the people were to give a loud shout, and then the walls would fall down. This may have seemed like a strange way to knock down the city walls, but the people trusted God and did exactly what He asked them to do, and the walls fell down.

Read and Share Together

Let's Talk about It!
★ What did God ask His people to do at the walls of Jericho?
★ What happened when the people trusted God and did as He said?

Share God's Love
CRASH!!! How would you have felt if you had been one of the Israelites when those huge walls around Jericho came tumbling down? Stories like this help us know that we can trust God to always do what's best for us. Here's a game about trust.

THE TRUST GAME

You'll need a blindfold and a partner. Wear the blindfold and let your partner guide you through a yard, playground, house, or apartment without running you into anything. Then switch roles. Did you or your partner have trouble trusting each other not to run into anything?

Prayer
Dear Lord, help me to always believe You and trust Your Word even when I don't understand it. Amen.

The Best Help Possible

"Is anything too hard for the Lord? No!" —Genesis 18:14

Did you know that there is absolutely nothing too hard for God? He can do anything! And here's the best part: He wants to help you when tough times come your way. All you have to do is ask Him. He'll do what's best for you and those you pray for. That's what happened when Joshua and his army had a big, big problem.

Plod, Plod, Plod! That's a fun word to say. Let's say it again: *Plod!* When you plod, you keep going—even when what you are doing is really tough or takes a long time. We say that people running a long race must plod on, putting one foot in front of the other until the race has ended.

463

Joshua 10:1–14

After Joshua led God's people into the land God had promised them, the Israelite army fought many battles. One day Joshua and his army had been fighting hard, but the battle was not finished. Joshua and his army had not won—not yet.

They needed more time. Joshua needed God's help and said, "Sun, stand still. . . . Moon, stand still. . . ." And the sun and moon "stopped" until Joshua and his army had won the battle. That's what God did for His people.

Read and Share Together

Let's Talk about It!
* Is there anything too hard for God?
* Why did Joshua need God's help?
* What did God do for His people?

Share God's Love
Wow! Were you surprised at how God helped Joshua?
It's good to know that you can ask God to help you with
problems. But you can also ask Him to help others with their
problems. Here's something you can make for someone who
needs God's help. It's a prayer card.

PRAYER CARD

Find some colorful paper and fold it in half to open
like a book. On the outside draw a picture. On the
inside write, "I'm praying for you." Sign your name
and give it to the person who needs God's help.

Prayer
*Dear Lord, thank You for always being there to help me
when I need You. I know You can do anything. Amen.*

You're a Winner!

We will shout for joy when you succeed. We will raise a flag in the name of our God. —PSALM 20:5

You've probably been a winner more times than you can remember. Everyone has victories where they have worked hard to win a game or overcome a fear or solve a problem. Some victories are large like the first time we spend the night away from home. Some victories are small like when we remember to pick up our toys. One of the best victories of all is the one Jesus gave us over sin—over the wrong things we do.

> Long ago the winners of contests, sports, or other such things were given a crown of leaves. Make a victory crown out of paper. Take turns wearing the crown with friends. Whoever is wearing the crown tells a story about a problem he or she overcame.

Judges 6:11–24; 6:33–7:8; 7:16–22

Gideon was a warrior God chose to save the people of Israel from their enemy, the Midianites. God sent an angel to tell Gideon what was going to happen and what God wanted him to do. Gideon was pretty sure God had the wrong man because Gideon was the least important member of his family. Gideon was scared. But God told Gideon He would be with him. So Gideon got a big army together. "Too many," said God. Gideon sent thousands of soldiers home. "Too many still," said God, until there were only 300 men.

Then Gideon gave each man a trumpet and a jar with a burning torch inside each jar. Gideon and his men quietly went to the edge of the camp where the enemy was sleeping. His men blew their trumpets, broke the jars, let their torches shine, and shouted, "For the Lord and for Gideon!" It scared the enemy so much they began to fight each other and run away. Gideon won the battle! Hooray, Gideon! Hooray, God!

Read and Share Together

Let's Talk about It!

★ What job did God choose Gideon to do?
★ What did Gideon's men do with the trumpets, jars, and torches?
★ What did the enemy do?

Share God's Love

Can you imagine winning a battle without fighting? God helped Gideon be victorious, and He can help you too. What are some things God has helped you overcome? Now name some new challenges you want to be victorious over. Here are some hints:

✢ Memorizing a Bible verse
✢ Learning a sport
✢ Eating your vegetables
✢ Making a new friend

Prayer

Dear Lord, thank You for giving me victory over sin. And help me remember to ask for Your help when I have a problem. Amen.

God Answers Prayer

"Give thanks to the Lord and pray to him." —1 Chronicles 16:8

Did you know that God answers *all* our prayers? Sometimes it may not seem like it, but He does. God's answer might be yes, or it might be no. He might answer us right away, or He might not answer our prayer for a long time. The Bible tells us about Hannah, who wanted something so much that she could hardly think about anything else. When God answered Hannah's prayer, she sang a song of thanks.

HANNAH'S SONG

"The Lord has filled
 my heart with joy.
I feel very strong
 in the Lord.
I can laugh at my enemies.
I am glad because
 you have helped me!"
—1 Samuel 2:1 (excerpt)

471

1 Samuel 1:1–2:2; 2:18–21

Hannah had no children, and that made her very sad. One day she went to God's Holy Tent, where she asked God to give her a baby son. Eli, the priest, saw her praying. Hannah told him she was very sad and talking to God about her troubles. Hannah promised that if God gave her a son, he would work for God all his life.

God answered Hannah's prayer. She named her son Samuel because Samuel sounds like the Hebrew word for "God heard." Hannah kept her promise, and Samuel worked for God all his life.

Read and Share Together

Let's Talk about It!
★ Who prayed and asked God for a child?
★ What did Hannah promise God?

Share God's Love
Have you ever been like Hannah and wanted something so much you could hardly think of anything else? A fun way to see how God answers your prayers is to make a prayer book. Fold some blank pieces of paper in half and staple them together to make a book. Decorate the cover of your prayer book. Inside write your prayers and date them. When God answers your prayer, write a thank-you to God and date it too. You can also draw or paste pictures of the people or things you pray about.

> ### REMEMBER . . .
>
> Sometimes God's answer is yes. Sometimes God's answer is no. And sometimes God's answer is "Not right now." God loves you so much, He will answer with the answer that is the very best for you.

Prayer
Dear Lord, help me to pray often. I'm glad I can talk to You. Amen.

Shhhhhhhhhh!

"Speak, Lord. I am your servant, and I am listening."
—1 SAMUEL 3:10

How well do you listen? Do you pay attention to what your parents and teachers say? Listening carefully is a good way to learn new things. God wants us to listen to His Word so we'll know what He wants us to do. For fun, play the Whispering Game to find out how well you listen.

THE WHISPERING GAME

In the Whispering Game, one person whispers a sentence only once to the person closest to his or her left. That person then whispers the sentence exactly to the person closest to his or her left and so it goes until the last person hears the sentence and says it out loud. Then the person who started the sentence repeats exactly what he or she said. Did the last person hear what the first person said? Try it again. This time the person who was last whispers a new sentence.

1 Samuel 3:1–14

Samuel was a boy who lived in God's Holy Tent. His job was to help Eli, the priest. One night Samuel was asleep when he heard someone call his name. He thought it was Eli. He got up and ran to Eli's bed. "I didn't call you," Eli said. "Go back to bed." So Samuel did.

Soon he heard the voice again. Samuel ran to Eli's bed again. After this happened three times, Eli knew God was calling Samuel. Eli said, "If you hear the voice again, Samuel, say, 'Speak, Lord. I am listening.'" And that is what Samuel did.

Read and Share Together

Let's Talk about It!
★ Who did Samuel think called him in the night?
★ What did Eli tell Samuel the third time Samuel woke him up?
★ What happened the fourth time Samuel heard someone call his name?

Share God's Love
What do you think Samuel would say about the noisy world we live in? Our world is so noisy, we don't always listen to the sounds around us. Sit very quietly and listen. What noises do you hear?

❖ A TV
❖ A radio
❖ A computer
❖ What else?

Ask permission to turn off as many sounds as you can. Sit quietly and think about all the wonderful things God has done. Pray and listen. God speaks to us through the Bible. And He speaks so our minds and hearts know what He is saying to us.

Prayer
Dear Lord, teach me to be quiet and listen to what You have to tell me as I read the Bible and pray. Amen.

Hooray for the Little Guy!

"Don't be afraid, because I am your God. I will make you strong and will help you." —ISAIAH 41:10

Have you ever been afraid to try something new? Ask God to give you the courage to be brave like the little kite in the following poem.

HOW THE LITTLE KITE LEARNED TO FLY

"I can never do it," the little kite said,
As he looked around at the others high over his head.
"I know I should fall if I tried to fly."
"Try," said the big kite, "only try!
Or I fear you never will learn at all."
But the little kite said, "I'm afraid I'll fall."

. . . .

Then the little kite's paper stirred
*   at the sight,*
And trembling he shook himself
*   free for flight.*
First whirling and frightened,
*   then braver grown,*
Up, up he rose through the air alone.

. . . .

"Oh, how happy I am!"
*   the little kite cried,*
"And all because I was brave,
*   and tried."*
—Unknown (excerpt)

Bible Story

1 Samuel 17:1–58

David was a shepherd. His job was to look after his father's sheep. Some people may have thought he was just "the little guy." One day his dad sent him to take some food to his brothers who were soldiers in a war. When David got to the battle line, he couldn't believe his eyes! All the soldiers were afraid of a giant named Goliath who was yelling across the valley for God's people to send a warrior out to fight him. No one would go.

Then David said, "I'll go!"

"No, no!" the king said.

But David was full of the courage God had given him. "God will win this battle for me," he said. David gathered five smooth stones and placed them in his pouch. Then with his slingshot in one hand, off he went to fight the giant. The giant was disgusted when he saw that David was just a boy.

David put a stone in the slingshot and whirled it around. The stone flew toward the giant and hit him in the head. The giant toppled to the ground. God had given David the courage to fight Goliath and win the battle.

Read and Share Together

Let's Talk about It!
★ Who were the soldiers afraid of?
★ Did David have a big weapon to fight Goliath?
★ How did God help David win the battle?

Share God's Love

Everyone needs courage doing something. David was courageous about facing a big giant. What do you need courage doing? Just for fun . . .

✦ Would it take more courage to jump into a swimming pool or to wear your pajamas backward?
✦ Would you rather say a poem in front of a group or go into a dark room?

With your family, take turns talking about how God gave each of you the courage to do something you had been afraid to do.

Prayer

Dear Lord, I really want to be brave, but sometimes I feel like that little kite. It's hard to try something new. Help me to have courage. Amen.

Friends Forever

A friend loves you all the time. —PROVERBS 17:17

Friends are good to have when you are happy and when you are sad, when you play and when you rest. Did you know that God is always your friend? Here is a poem about friendship. Let's read it together.

FRIENDSHIP

You are my friend
and I am yours.
We play inside
and out of doors.

When I am sad
You hold my hand.
When you are sad
I understand.

Friends forever,
I hope we'll be,
'Til we're at least
A hundred and three.
—Gwen Ellis

Now find out about
two best friends in the Bible.

1 Samuel 18:1–16; 20

David and Jonathan were best friends. Jonathan's father, Saul, was king of Israel. Prince Jonathan would have been the next king, but God had chosen David instead. The people loved David. That made King Saul angry and jealous. He was afraid of David and wanted to kill him. Jonathan heard about his father's plan and warned David. Then he helped David run far away where no one could hurt him. Jonathan even gave David his coat to wear.

Read and Share Together

Let's Talk about It!
- ★ Who was Jonathan's best friend?
- ★ Who was Jonathan's father?
- ★ Why was King Saul angry and jealous?

Share God's Love

David must have thought about his friend every time he looked at the coat Jonathan gave him. Here's a fun thing to do with your friends to show your friendship.

FRIENDSHIP

Make a friendship bracelet out of a single piece of ribbon, embroidery floss, beautiful thread, or paper chains. Before cutting, carefully measure a piece of ribbon around your friend's wrist so it will fit loosely. Remove it from the wrist, add four inches (or enough to allow you to tie a knot), then cut the ribbon. Now place it back around your friend's wrist, and tie a double-knot so the bracelet fits loosely. Ask a grown-up to cut the ribbon ends near to the knot. *TA-DA!* You made a friendship bracelet!

Prayer
Dear Lord, bless my friends and help us be true friends like Jonathan and David. Amen.

Be Kind

Don't ever stop being kind and truthful. Let kindness and truth show in all you do. —PROVERBS 3:3

Have you ever let a friend go first to play with a new game or toy? Hooray for you! Did you know that when you show kindness it not only makes others happy, it makes God happy too?

When Timmy's mom first told him they were going to help Mrs. Cobb, an elderly lady from their church, he thought it would be boring. But he was wrong! Mrs. Cobb tells wonderful stories and makes yummy pies. Timmy looks forward to spending time with her. He shows kindness by being polite and helping her by doing things like holding the car door open. Being kind is a good way to show God's love.

487

Bible Story

1 Samuel 31; 2 Samuel 1:1–4; 5:1–4; 9

Long ago David's best friend, Jonathan, died. After David became king, he wanted to show kindess to Jonathan by helping anyone who was still alive in Saul's family. David learned that Jonathan's son Mephibosheth (*mef-ee-bo'-sheth*) was crippled in both feet and living in Lo Debar. David was very kind to Mephibosheth. He treated Jonathan's son as if he were one of his own sons and always let him eat at his table. He also made sure that all of Jonathan's property was returned to Mephibosheth and that the land was farmed, so Mephibosheth would always have food to eat. Mephibosheth lived in Jerusalem, and David took care of him his whole life. David was kind.

489

Read and Share Together

Let's Talk about It!

★ Who is Mephibosheth?

★ How did David show kindness to Mephibosheth?

Share God's Love

If you were Mephibosheth, how would David's kindness make you feel? Are your manners as nice as David's? Here's a fun quiz on kindness.

KINDNESS QUIZ

[Answer True or False]

1. When someone does something nice for you, you should say nothing.
2. When you are finished with dinner, it is kind to help with the dishes.
3. When you receive a gift, you should say, "Thank you."
4. When you see a line of kids waiting their turn for a ride, it is kind to push them out of the way and jump in the ride first.

[1. F / 2. T / 3. T / 4. F]

Prayer

Dear Lord, I want to be a kind child and think of others first. Please help me use good manners. Amen.

490

Let's Share

"Do for other people the same things you want them to do for you." —Matthew 7:12

Tina pulled an apple from her backpack. "Want to share?" she asked Cindy. She did, but Cindy's little brothers wanted some too. What should the girls do? Here's a hint: God wants us to treat others the same way we want to be treated. Read the story below for another hint.

Jennie didn't want to share her toys. Jennie didn't realize how her selfish behavior made her friends feel until one day when she went to Fran's house to play. When Jennie wanted to play with Fran's beautiful dollhouse, Fran wouldn't let her. Jennie didn't like not being allowed to play with the dollhouse. Right then she decided she would treat her friends like she wanted to be treated. Now Jennie and her friends have lots more fun.

491

1 Kings 17:1–16

Times were hard in Israel. The people had not been faithful to God and He was not sending them rain. So God put Elijah near a stream where he would have water to drink and where birds fed him bread and meat. But after a while the stream dried up. Then God told Elijah to go to a certain woman and ask her for food.

Elijah went and asked. The woman said she only had enough flour and oil for one more meal for her son and herself, and then they would die of hunger. Elijah told her to cook for him first and she would be all right. Because she had a sharing heart, she did what Elijah asked and cooked him a piece of bread. Guess what? God made her food last so that the woman, her son, and Elijah would eat until once again there was food in the land.

Read and Share Together

Let's Talk about It!
* What did God tell Elijah to do?
* What did the woman do to help Elijah?
* What did God provide for the woman, her son, and Elijah?

Share God's Love

When the woman gave Elijah food, she was doing something God wants us all to do: She was sharing! She was treating Elijah the same way she'd want to be treated.

Here's a fun way to start thinking about things you can share. Start by drawing a heart shape on a piece of paper. Next draw lines across it to divide it into four parts. In each part, draw a picture of something that is hard for you to share but that you will begin sharing to please God. Talk with your family about ways you can begin sharing. Then decide what you will do the next time you are asked to share. Now you have a sharing heart.

Prayer
*Dear God, help me learn to share with others
as You want me to. Amen.*

Fire from Heaven

Pray with all kinds of prayers, and ask for everything you need.
—EPHESIANS 6:18

Every day you talk to lots of people—your family, friends, teachers, and maybe even your teddy bear. But did you know that God wants you to talk to Him every day too? When you talk to God, it's called prayer. And you can talk to Him anytime, anywhere. God can help us with our problems, big or small—all we need to do is ask. We don't need to yell or scream.

Julius wanted a bear.
He wanted it NOW!
He wouldn't share.
He yelled, he stomped,
and threw a fit.
In a loud voice said,
"I deserve it!"

Mom wasn't pleased.
God was unhappy too.
His sister got the bear.
And she said, "Thank you!"
—Laura Minchew

In today's Bible story, find out what mighty thing happened when Elijah talked to God.

1 Kings 18:1, 15–46

After about three years with no rain, the people of Israel were desperate for water. So all 450 prophets who prayed to the false god called Baal met Elijah—a prophet of the only real God—on a mountaintop. The group of prophets built an altar to Baal, placed wood on it, and then placed an offering of meat on top of the wood. Elijah did the same, but his altar was to God.

The prophets yelled and screamed from morning until evening as they begged Baal to answer them and send fire. No answer came. No fire came. (This is because Baal is not a god. There is only one God. Do you know who it is?)

Now it was Elijah's turn. He had people pour water on the wood and the offering of meat until the altar was soaked. The people knew it was too wet for a fire to light. Next Elijah asked the real God to answer by sending fire to burn the wet offering! Just like that, God sent fire that burned up the entire altar. Wow! God had answered Elijah's prayer and proved that He was the real God.

Read and Share Together

Let's Talk about It!

* How long had the people of Israel been without rain?
* What did the prophets of the false god Baal do?
* What did Elijah do when it was his turn?

Share God's Love

Isn't it good to know that you can talk to God about anything? He's interested in everything you think and feel. Did something exciting happen to you? Tell God. We all have good days and not-so-good days! What kind of day is it when . . .

✦ You fall down in a mud puddle?
✦ You learn something new?
✦ You scrape your knee?
✦ You go for a swim in a pool full of Jell-O?

Prayer

Dear God, I know You are a mighty God who can do anything. That is why I pray to You. Thank You for hearing my prayers. Amen.

An Honest Person

"Tell each other the truth." —Zechariah 8:16

Do you always tell the truth and try to do the right thing? Would you return a wallet you found—even if it had money in it? Sometimes it might seem that telling lies and not being honest is easier than telling the truth. But God wants us to tell the truth.

Did you know that one of the presidents of the United States was such an honest person he was called "Honest Abe"? His real name was Abraham Lincoln. It is believed that he got this nickname when he worked as a clerk in a store as a young man. One day he gave a customer incorrect change. When he discovered his mistake, Lincoln walked a long way to give the person the right change.

In today's Bible story, we'll see how lies led to some really bad things.

1 Kings 21–22:39

One day King Ahab went to his neighbor, Naboth, and asked for his land to plant a vegetable garden. Naboth said, "No." It made the king very angry. When he told his wife, Queen Jezebel, what had happened, she got very angry too.

So the queen made a plan that would help them get Naboth's land. At that time, speaking badly against God or the king was against the law. Queen Jezebel got some people to say that Naboth had said bad things about God and the king.

The king and queen knew it was a lie, but they let Naboth be killed for something he didn't do, just to get his land.

Later, King Ahab and Queen Jezebel both died terrible deaths because of all the lies and evil things they had done.

Read and Share Together

Let's Talk about It!

★ What did King Ahab and Queen Jezebel want?
★ What did they do to get it?
★ What happened to King Ahab and Queen Jezebel?

Share God's Love

Ugh! That story didn't have a happy ending. But God wants us to know that lies and wrongdoing can hurt others and the liars and wrongdoers too. Share God's love by always telling the truth and being honest with everyone you meet. If you have told a lie, ask for forgiveness from the person you lied to. Play this game to see how good you are at knowing whether or not someone is telling a lie.

> ### THE TRUTH GAME
>
> Take turns being the speaker. The speaker can choose to tell the truth or a lie. The rest of the people in the room guess whether the speaker was telling the truth or a lie. Who guessed right the most often?

Prayer

Dear Lord, help me to always tell the truth. Amen.

Faithful

"If you are faithful, I will give you the crown of life."
—Revelation 2:10

In Yellowstone Park there is an amazing feature called Old Faithful Geyser. Perhaps you've seen it. It is a hole in the ground that shoots hot water into the air every 60 to 90 minutes. No one knows how long the geyser has been doing this or when it was discovered, but it got its name in 1879 because of how it faithfully spouted hot water, which it's still doing today.

You can see Old Faithful for yourself. Ask a grownup to help you search the Internet for Yellowstone Park's Web site. Within the park menu, click on Old Faithful.

In today's Bible story, we'll read about Elijah, one of God's faithful followers. God wants us to be faithful by living for Him every day too.

503

2 Kings 2:1–12

Elijah was a faithful servant of God. He stayed true to God even though he was threatened by a wicked queen and had to hide out in the desert. As he got older, Elijah continued to serve God faithfully. He trained his helper Elisha to do the same thing. Elisha went everywhere with Elijah until one day something amazing happened.

Fiery horses and a chariot of fire came down from heaven, and—
WHOOSH!—a whirlwind carried Elijah straight up to heaven. He was
faithful to God right to the end, and God was faithful to bring Elijah
right up to heaven to be with Him forever.

Read and Share Together

Let's Talk about It!
* What kind of a servant of God was Elijah?
* Where did Elijah go in the whirlwind?

Share God's Love
Wow! Isn't it amazing how God took Elijah to heaven? And it's good to know that one day we, too, can go to heaven by being God's faithful followers. How faithful are you? Try this quiz.

> **YOU ARE BEING FAITHFUL TO GOD WHEN YOU . . .**
>
> [Answer True or False]
>
> 1. Do what is right.
> 2. Tell the truth.
> 3. Tell a lie.
> 4. Follow God even during tough times.

[1.T / 2.T / 3. F / 4.T]

Prayer
Dear Lord, I'm just learning about being faithful. Help me be loyal, true, and dependable in everything I do. Amen.

God Provides

Praise the Lord, day by day. God our Savior helps us.
—Psalm 68:19

How many names do you have? Think about it. You have your given first name and maybe a middle name. You have a last name and maybe a nickname. You might be called son or daughter, niece or nephew, grandson or granddaughter. Sometimes what you are called tells something about you.

Did you know that God has several names that describe Him too? One of God's names means "The Lord provides." The Lord gives us what we need. Sometimes He does that by providing others to help us. In today's Bible story, we'll see how God used Elisha to provide the help someone needed.

God has sent people to help you too. These people might be called mom, dad, grandma, grandpa, aunt, uncle, brother, sister, teacher, or friend. Quick, name as many people as you can who God has sent to help you. **Ready, set, GO!**

507

2 Kings 4:1–7

A woman went to Elisha, the prophet of God, for help. She was very upset. Her husband had died, and he owed another man a lot of money. That man was going to take the woman's two sons and make them slaves, unless she could pay what her husband owed him. Elisha asked the woman what she had in her house. The woman said, "I have nothing but a small pot of oil."

Elisha told her to get all the empty jars she could borrow from her neighbors. "Take your small pot of oil and begin pouring it into all the empty jars," Elisha told her. The woman did as he said. She poured and poured and poured until every jar was full. Then the woman took the jars and sold the oil to pay her debt. Now her sons got to stay at home with her, and they had plenty of money to live on. Hooray! God had provided for her.

Read and Share Together

Let's Talk about It!
* What was the woman's problem?
* What did Elisha tell her to do?
* What did God do for her and her sons?

Share God's Love
A pot of oil! Who would have known that was all the woman and her sons needed? But God knew, and He sent Elisha to help her. Today God still sends people to help others. God sends people like you to provide what others need. Sometimes what a person needs is something as small as someone to open a door. Sometimes it's very big, like someone to adopt a child or bring food to those who are hungry. You never know how God will use you to help others, but you can be sure He will.

> Name five ways God has used you
> and your family to help others.

Prayer
Dear Lord, I'm glad You provide for my needs. Please use me to help others whenever I can. Amen.

Achoo!

I praise you because you made me in an
amazing and wonderful way. —Psalm 139:14

God created sneezes to protect us. There is a wonderful story in the
Bible about a little boy who sneezed a big sneeze. Who do you suppose
it was? And why was a sneeze so important? Read the Bible story on the
next page to find out.

FACTS ABOUT SNEEZES

- You sneeze to clear your breathing passages.
- Your whole body gets into it? Your nose tickles, your brain tells
  you to sneeze, and your muscles get ready for the big event.
- Most people close their eyes when they sneeze. Do you?
- You sneeze at the smell of pepper.
- The speed of a sneeze can be more than 100 miles per hour!

Bible Story

2 Kings 4:8–37

Elisha often stayed with a Shunammite woman, her husband, and their young son. The family had even built a special room for Elisha on the roof of their house.

One day, the little boy became sick when he went out in the field where his father was harvesting grain. They took the little boy home, but there was nothing anyone could do. The little boy died. The Shunammite woman placed the boy on Elisha's bed. She hurried to get Elisha to bring him to help her little boy. Elisha went with the lady back to her house and prayed. Then all of a sudden, *"Achoo!"* The little boy sneezed. Then he sneezed six more times and opened his eyes. It was a miracle. God had brought the little boy back to life.

Read and Share Together

Let's Talk about It!

★ What happened to the little boy?

★ What did God do when Elisha prayed for the little boy?

Share God's Love

Has anyone ever said, "God bless you!" when you sneezed? Many people do, and it's always a good way to share God's love, because it's like saying a prayer for someone.

FUNNY SNEEZES

On a piece of paper, draw as many round circles as there are people in your family. Put eyes on each of the circles. Now think about how each person sneezes. Draw a mouth and nose to show that person's sneeze. How funny does it look? Did you remember to draw a picture of yourself?

Prayer

Dear Lord, You are the One who gave me my breath and my sneezes. Thank You for my amazing body. Amen.

The Borrowed Ax

Do not be interested only in your own life, but
be interested in the lives of others. —PHILIPPIANS 2:4

How do you feel when you lose something? Are you sad? What if you
had borrowed what you lost from a friend? Now the friend it belonged
to will be sad too. When we borrow something, we should take care
of it as if it were the most important thing we ever had—whether it is
something very small or very big, whether it cost a lot of money or none
at all. In the Bible story on the next page, a man was
very sad when he lost something he had borrowed.
See what God's prophet Elisha did to
help the man.

515

2 Kings 6:1–7

Long ago work tools were made by hand, and tools were expensive and rare. One day some prophets were chopping down trees with heavy axes to build them a place to live. While they were working, a man gave a strong chop to a tree with an ax. When he did that, the heavy iron axhead flew off the handle and went right into the water. It quickly sank.

"Oh no," said the man, "I borrowed that ax." He was sad. He wouldn't be able to return the ax to its owner.

Elisha, the prophet, was there. He asked, "Where did it fall?" The man showed him. Elisha cut a stick and threw it into the water, and the heavy iron axhead floated to the surface. The man who lost it picked it up. It was a miracle.

Read and Share Together

Let's Talk about It!
* What happened to one man's ax while chopping down trees?
* What did Elisha do?
* What floated to the water's surface?

Share God's Love
Do you think the axhead would have been able to float to the top without Elisha's help? Try this experiment.

> ### THE SINKING PENNY
>
> You'll need a clear glass or plastic cup, clear water, and a penny. Fill the glass three-quarters full of water. Place the glass where everyone can see it. Drop the penny in the glass. Did the penny float? An axhead is much heavier than a penny. Share God's love by telling someone about the amazing miracle of the floating axhead.

Prayer
Dear Lord, help me take care of anything I borrow from others as if it were my own. I want to take good care of everything I use. Thank You, Lord. Amen.

I Choose You

"Who knows, you may have been chosen queen for just such a time as this." —ESTHER 4:14

Have you ever been chosen to do something special? It can be lots of fun, but sometimes it can be a little scary too. Maybe you were chosen to help a teacher, or tell about a trip you made, or sing a song, or be on a team to play a game. Let's read together the Bible story on the next page and find out about a beautiful, young queen who was chosen by God for a very big job. She lived in Persia, which today we know as Iran. If you want to know where that is, ask someone to help you find it on a map.

Esther 1–9

Esther was an ordinary girl living in Persia. Then God chose her for an extraordinary job. First she became queen of the land. But after she was queen, one of the king's men wanted to do away with all God's people.

Esther's cousin Mordecai came to her. He knew that God could use Esther to save God's people. He told her, "It could be that God has made you queen for just this time."

What Esther did next was very courageous. Even though the king could have killed her, she went to the king and asked him to save her people. The king did what she asked. Yea, Esther!

Read and Share Together

Let's Talk about It!
* Where did Esther live?
* What did God choose her to do?
* What happened when she did what God asked?

Share God's Love

God chooses people to get His work done. You can share God's love by helping to do His work on earth. What are some ways you can help God with His work?

❖ Maybe you could give some of your toys to someone who doesn't have any.
❖ Maybe there is something you could do to help your parents, your grandparents, and even your brothers and sisters.

What else can you think of that can help God with His work? Ask a grownup to help you make a plan. Then do the work. You'll be glad you did.

Prayer
Dear Lord, help me to think of things I can do to be Your helper. Amen.

The Right Time

There is a right time for everything. —ECCLESIASTES 3:1

When you have choices to make, do you ever have a hard time deciding what's most important? Everything has an order—even your shoes and socks. What would happen if you put on your shoes and then your socks? That wouldn't work, would it? So the best choice is to put on your socks and then your shoes. Now, if you had to choose between watching your favorite TV program or doing your homework, which one should you do first? The Bible tells us that there is a right time for everything God has given us to do.

BEDTIME ORDER

For fun, number these bedtime things in the best order.

___Get in bed.
___Have sweet dreams.
___Brush your teeth.
___Eat a snack.
___Say your prayers.

Ecclesiastes 3:1–8

A wise man said in the Bible that there is a right time for everything in life. Some things we can't choose, such as when to be born. But other things we can choose, such as when to be silent and when to speak or when to hug and when not to hug or when to be happy and when to be sad. God wants us to make good choices about our time and to let Him take care of those things we can't make happen or fix or change. He is in control of everything.

Read and Share Together

Let's Talk about It!
★ What does the Bible say about the time for things?
★ What kind of choices does God want us to make?

Share God's Love
Isn't it great that there is a time for everything! There's a time to be awake and a time to go to sleep. There is a time to go places and a time to stay home. There is a time to work and a time to play.

> ### IT'S TIME
>
> Draw some clocks for your room. These can be clocks with hands or digital clocks. Each clock should show the time you or your family do something. Write over your clock what you do at this time. Is it eat dinner? Go to church? Go to bed? Make as many clocks as you need.

Prayer
Dear Lord, please help my family and me to make good choices about what we are doing. Amen.

God's Angels Watch Over You

"Don't think these little children are worth nothing.
I tell you that they have angels in heaven who are
always with my Father in heaven." —Matthew 18:10

Did you know that God sends His angels to watch over us? God promises in the Bible that He will put His angels in charge of you. Let's read together His promise below.

He has put his angels in charge of you.
They will watch over you wherever you go. . . .
The Lord says, "If someone loves me,
*   I will save him.*
I will protect those who know me.
They will call to me, and I will
*   answer them.*
I will be with them in trouble.
I will rescue them and
*   honor them.*
I will give them a long,
*   full life.*
They will see how I can save."
—Psalm 91:11, 14–16

Now check out today's Bible story to see how God's angel helped Daniel.

Daniel 6:11–28

Daniel was a man who loved God with all his heart. He prayed to God three times a day. The king was planning to put Daniel in charge of the whole kingdom. This made some leaders jealous, and they tricked the king into throwing Daniel into a hungry lions' den.

But God sent His angel to take care of Daniel. The angel closed the lions' jaws so they couldn't bite Daniel.

In the morning, the king had Daniel removed from the lions' den. Daniel was not hurt at all, because he had trusted in God.

Read and Share Together

Let's Talk about It!
* ★ What happened to Daniel?
* ★ Who did God send to help Daniel?

Share God's Love
To share God's love, make paper angels for your family and friends and tell them how God's angels are watching over us. For each angel, you'll need two round coffee filters, glue, coloring crayons, and a little stiff paper or felt. Ask a grownup to help.

1. **Wings:** Fold one filter in half and put to the side.
2. **Angel's body:** Fold the second filter in half, then fold the sides back so the edges meet in the center to form a cone shape. Glue together. With the first filter's folded edge at the top, glue it to the back of the cone—so that the top of the cone is below the center point of the wings.
3. **Angel's face:** Cut a small circle from stiff paper or felt and draw a face on it. Glue to the top of the cone.

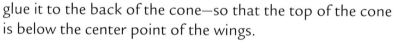

Prayer

Dear Lord, thank You for sending angels to watch over me. Even though I may not see them, I know they are there because Your Word tells me so. Amen.

I Will Obey

Children, obey your parents in all things.
This pleases the Lord. —COLOSSIANS 3:20

Have your parents ever asked you to do something you really didn't want to do? Did you do it anyway just because they asked you? If so, good for you! That was obeying. Here's a fun way to see what else you know about obeying.

THE FUN OBEYING QUIZ
[Answer True or False]

1. When children disobey, they usually get ice cream.
2. Grownups do not have to follow the rules.
3. God wants children to obey their parents.
4. God wants everyone to obey Him.
5. Rules are made to keep us all safe.

[1. F / 2. F / 3. T / 4. T / 5. T]

Bible Story

Jonah 1–3:10

God told Jonah to go to Nineveh and preach to the people. But Jonah didn't like those people, so he disobeyed God and got on a ship going the opposite direction from Nineveh. At sea, a terrible storm was about to sink the ship. Everyone was afraid.

Jonah told the sailors to throw him overboard, and the storm would stop. That's what they did, and the storm did stop! A large fish quickly swallowed Jonah.

God let Jonah stay in the belly of that stinky old fish for three days, until Jonah prayed to Him saying he would obey.

Then that fish spit Jonah up on dry land. And Jonah went straight to Nineveh and preached to the people.

533

Read and Share Together

Let's Talk about It!
★ Why did Jonah choose not to obey God?
★ What did Jonah do?
★ What made Jonah change his mind about obeying God?

Share God's Love
Sometimes we're like Jonah; we don't want to do what God asks. But God always has a good reason for everything. He knows everything about you. He knows what's best. Obeying God is a great way to show that you love Him. Now for fun try this game that can only be won by obeying.

SIMON SAYS

To play, one person is Simon or "it." Simon stands in front of everyone. No one moves until Simon tells him or her what to do. When Simon gives a command (like "Simon says turn in a circle"), everyone must follow the command. But if Simon gives a command (like "turn in a circle") without saying "Simon says," no one should move—and if someone does move, that person is out. The last person still in the game is the most obedient.

Prayer
Dear God, help me to obey—even when I don't want to. Amen.

God's Family

The Father has loved us so much . . . that we
are called children of God. —1 John 3:1

There are all kinds of families. How would you describe your family? Families are important to God. They are so important to Him that even though He could have sent His Son to earth as a grown man, He didn't. He sent Jesus as a little baby to be part of an earthly family with Mary as His mother and Joseph as His father.

Did you know that anyone who believes in Jesus can be part of God's family? Wow! That's one big family! Think of everyone you're related to when you join God's family. You could count for hours, days, months, even years, and still not name them all!

Bible Story

Luke 1:26–2:52; John 19:25–27; Matthew 1:18–2:23

When God was ready to send His Son to the world, He chose Mary and Joseph, a couple who were about to get married. He sent an angel to tell Mary that she was going to have a baby. Then God sent an angel to talk to Joseph and tell him he should make a home for Mary and the baby. Jesus was born in Bethlehem, where shepherds and wise men came to honor Him.

Later Jesus lived in Nazareth where Mary and Joseph took care of Him until He was grown. And Jesus obeyed them as His parents. He never forgot them and the safe place they had made for Him to live. Even as He was dying on the Cross, Jesus was thinking about His mother.

537

Read and Share Together

Let's Talk about It!

★ Who were Jesus' parents on earth?
★ How did Jesus act toward Mary and Joseph?

Share God's Love

Isn't it good to know that you can be part of God's family? For fun make a family tree showing some of the people from the Bible who are also children of God. Remember to include yourself. Here's an example:

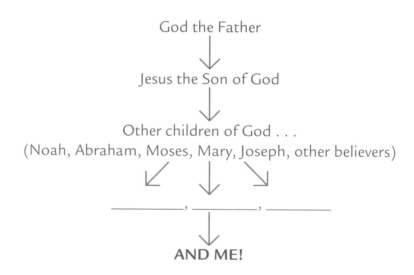

God the Father

↓

Jesus the Son of God

↓

Other children of God . . .
(Noah, Abraham, Moses, Mary, Joseph, other believers)

↙   ↓   ↘

_____ , _____ , _____

↓

AND ME!

Prayer

Dear Lord, thank You for making a great big family of those who believe, and inviting us all to be a part of Your family. Amen.

Jesus' Birthday

Thanks be to God for his gift that is too wonderful to explain.
—2 CORINTHIANS 9:15

When you think about Christmas, do you think about trees and presents? Did you know that Christmas is the time when many Christians celebrate the birth of Jesus? That's right, they're having a big birthday party for Jesus! Long ago, when Jesus was born, some shepherds got the news from a messenger of God, an angel! We still sing about what the angels said today. Sing the song below.

ANGELS WE HAVE
HEARD ON HIGH

Come to Bethlehem and see
Him Whose birth the angels sing,
Come, adore on bended knee,
Christ the Lord, the newborn King.
—James Chadwick (excerpt)

In today's Bible story, find out what the shepherds thought when they first saw the angel and how they found the baby Jesus.

Bible Story

Luke 2:8–20

The best news in the whole world came to shepherds who were watching over their sheep. Suddenly, an angel in a bright light appeared to tell them something wonderful. When the shepherds first saw the angel, they were afraid.

"Don't be afraid," the angel said. "I have good news for you. Your Savior was born in Bethlehem tonight. He's Christ the Lord. You will find Him lying in a feeding box."

Then a very large group of angels joined the first angel. They all were praising God. When the angels went back to heaven, the shepherds went to Bethlehem and found Mary and Joseph and saw the baby lying in a feeding box. It was just as the angel had told them.

Read and Share Together

Let's Talk about It!
★ Who heard the news of Jesus' birth while watching sheep?
★ Who told them?

Share God's Love
Christmas is one of the best times of the year to share God's love. Make Christmas cards to share with your family and friends. On your cards, draw pictures of

❖ angels,
❖ the shepherds,
❖ baby Jesus.

Your cards will tell others about the good news of Jesus' birth. If others are making cards with you, take turns talking about what each of you might have thought if you had been one of the shepherds and an angel appeared before you.

Prayer
Dear Jesus, thank You for coming to be my Savior. I love You. Amen.

542

God's Best Promise Comes True

"For God loved the world so much that he gave his only Son.
God gave his Son so that whoever believes in him
may not be lost, but have eternal life." —JOHN 3:16

Do you keep your promises? God keeps His. When God says something will happen, it will happen. God's best promise was that He would send His Son, Jesus, to us. He told us how Jesus would come to earth and what Jesus would do here. Every promise came true.

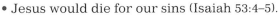

WHAT GOD PROMISED

- Jesus would be born in Bethlehem (Micah 5:2).
- Jesus would ride into Jerusalem on the colt of a donkey (Zechariah 9:9).
- Jesus would die for our sins (Isaiah 53:4–5).

543

Bible Story

Luke 2:1–7; 19:29–38; Matthew 27:35, 45–50

Mary and Joseph lived in Nazareth. Just before it was time for Jesus to be born, they had to go to Bethlehem. While they were there, Jesus was born—just as God had promised.

When Jesus was a grownup, He rode the colt of a donkey into Jerusalem. Crowds of His followers said, "God bless the king who comes in the name of the Lord!"

Later, Jesus was arrested and nailed to a cross where He died for our sins.

545

Read and Share Together

Let's Talk about It!
★ Where did Mary and Joseph live?
★ Where did God say Jesus would be born?
★ What happens when God makes a promise?

Share God's Love
Here's a fun way to share God's love. Make a promise book and write promises from the Bible in it. To get started look at God's promises in these Bible verses and write them down in your book.

John 3:16

1 John 1:9

Philippians 2:12

Proverbs 3:6

Psalm 46:1

Joshua 1:9

James 5:16

James 1:5

Prayer
Dear Lord, thank You for keeping Your promises. Help me learn more about You and Your promises. Amen.

One of God's Top Ten

Children, obey your parents the way the Lord wants.
This is the right thing to do. —EPHESIANS 6:1

Did you know that honoring your parents is one of God's top ten rules? So what does "honoring" mean? The answer is simple: You honor your parents when you do what they ask, follow the rules they make, and behave well—even when your parents are not in the room.

How well do you honor your parents? Answer the following questions yes or no:

1. Do you enjoy spending time with your parents?
2. Do you do what your parents ask you to do?
3. Do you say "please" and "thank you" to your parents and others?

If you answered every question "YES!" you are doing a great job of honoring your parents. If you answered any question "no," ask your parents what you can do to change that "no" into a "YES!"

547

Luke 2:41–52

When Jesus was 12 years old, He went with His parents to the Temple in Jerusalem. Soon it was time to go home to Nazareth. Everyone packed up and left.

At first Mary and Joseph thought Jesus was traveling with some of their family and friends. When they realized Jesus wasn't in the group, they went back to Jerusalem where they found Jesus talking with some religious teachers in the Temple just as if He was one of them.

When Mary and Joseph told Jesus it was time to go, He honored them by respectfully doing what they asked. He left the teachers and went home with Mary and Joseph. There He continued to learn and grow, to obey His parents, and to please God in all that He did.

Read and Share Together

Let's Talk about It!
★ What is God's rule about parents?
★ What was Jesus doing in the Temple?
★ How did Jesus honor His parents?

Share God's Love

Think about it! Jesus was once a kid like you with earthly parents. It's hard to imagine, isn't it? Honoring your parents is an easy way to be even more like Jesus. Do you know your parents' favorite words? They are:

"I LOVE YOU!"

Every mom and every dad likes to hear those words. Can you say them now and share a hug?

Prayer
Dear God, please help me be the child You want me to be and honor my parents. Amen.

Say No to Temptation

And now he [Jesus] can help those who are tempted . . . because he himself suffered and was tempted. —HEBREWS 2:18

When we are tempted, it is as if someone is tapping us on the shoulder to get us to do something we know we shouldn't do. If you've ever wanted to sneak a yummy cookie when you were told to wait, you've been tempted. If you've ever wanted to play with your friends when you were told to clean your room, you've been tempted.

It's no surprise that *everyone* is tempted. Even Jesus was tempted. See today's Bible story and find out how. The important thing is to turn away from temptation and DO THE RIGHT THING!

551

Matthew 4:1–11

When Jesus was tempted, He was out in the desert all alone. Jesus was very hungry and tired when Satan came to tempt Him to do some things that were wrong.

First Satan told Jesus to "turn these rocks into bread." But Jesus had studied God's Word, so He remembered what He had learned from the Scriptures. He said, "A person doesn't live just by eating bread. A person lives by doing everything the Lord says."

"Jump down from the top of the Temple. God's angels will catch you," said Satan. Jesus answered, "The Scriptures also say, 'Do not test God.'"

Then Satan took Jesus to the top of a tall mountain and showed Him all the kingdoms of the world. "Bow down and give honor to me, and I will give you all these things," said Satan. But Jesus said, "Go away from Me! It is written in the Scriptures, 'You must worship only the Lord God.'" And Satan left.

Read and Share Together

Let's Talk about It!
★ How was Jesus feeling when Satan came to Him?
★ Did Jesus do the right or the wrong thing?

Share God's Love
Like Jesus, you too can say "No!" to temptation. Here's a fun way to help you remember:

> Say, "No! No! No!" loud and clear,
> Don't pretend that you aren't here.
> You know right is right and wrong is wrong.
> Hear it, believe it, be strong.
> Throw out temptation as you should.
> Then bless the Lord for all that's good.
> —June Ford

Now share God's love with your family and friends by telling about three times you've said "No!" to temptation.

Prayer
Dear God, sometimes it is hard to do what is right. Please help me say no to temptation and to do the right thing. Amen.

When You're Sick

The prayer that is said with faith will make the sick person well.
The Lord will heal him. —James 5:15

Have you ever been sick? Yuck! It's no fun, is it? But we can ask Jesus today to heal us when we are sick. He knows what we need. He knows the doctors and medicines that will help us get well. He gives us family and friends who take care of us. He puts foods like fruits, vegetables, and grains on earth for us to eat. He gives us lots of ways to exercise like walking, running, jumping, and climbing. He provides us a way to relax our body through sleep. So even though we may not see Jesus, He can heal us. Read today's Bible story and see how Jesus healed a child He never saw.

Pretend that someone in your family is sick. It could be Mom, Dad, your brother or sister—even one of your toys. What do you need to do to take care of that person?

555

Bible Story

John 4:46–53

One day at exactly one o'clock in the afternoon, an important man in the government begged Jesus to come heal his son. The boy was very, very sick and in a different town. Jesus knew He didn't need to go there. He told the father, "Go home. Your son will live." The man believed Jesus and went home.

On the man's way home, his servants met him and told him his son was
well. The father asked what time his son began to get well. The servants
said, "Your son's fever went away at one o'clock yesterday." The father
knew that was the exact time Jesus had said, "Your son will live." Now
not only did the man believe in Jesus, all the people in his house believed
in Jesus too.

Read and Share Together

Let's Talk about It!
★ What did Jesus do when the man asked Him to heal his son?
★ Who believed in Jesus?

Share God's Love
No one likes to be sick, but it's good to know that Jesus can help us even if we can't see Him! For a little fun, see how well you know what to do to stay healthy.

> ### A HEALTH QUIZ
> [Answer True or False]
>
> To keep your body strong and healthy . . .
>
> 1. Eat candy and cookies three times a day.
> 2. Go to bed on time to let your body rest.
> 3. Put ice cream on your vegetables.
> 4. Exercise every day.
> 5. Ride your bike or play a game outside.
> 6. Never ever brush your teeth.

[1. F / 2. T / 3. F / 4. T / 5. T / 6. F]

Prayer
*Dear Lord, help me eat right and sleep well
so that I can stay well. Amen.*

Being a Helper

Trust the Lord and do good. —PSALM 37:3

You can be a helper whether you are very, very young or very, very old. Think of some of the many ways you can be a helper. In the story below, Laura thought of a way to be a big help to her mother.

Laura was a new big sister. One evening when her mother was making dinner, Laura thought of a way she could help. She got on the floor beside her baby brother and began to talk to him, making him smile and kick his feet. She kept him busy until dinner was ready.

"Thanks for being such a good helper, Laura!" her mother said.

Laura really liked being a helper.

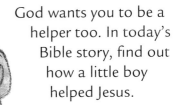

God wants you to be a helper too. In today's Bible story, find out how a little boy helped Jesus.

Bible Story

John 6:1–14; Matthew 14:13–21

One day a crowd of people followed Jesus to see His miracles and hear Him teach about God's love. By the time they reached Jesus, it was late in the day, and there were more than 5,000 hungry people. But there was no food, except for five small loaves of bread and two small fish that a boy had brought with him. The boy gave his bread and fish to Jesus' helpers.

Jesus thanked God for the boy's food and gave everyone there as much to eat as they wanted. It was a miracle. There were even 12 baskets of food left over!

Read and Share Together

Let's Talk about It!
★ How was the boy a helper?
★ What was in the boy's lunch?
★ What did Jesus do?

Share God's Love
You can be a good helper by making bread and fish sandwiches for lunch. One type of bread and fish sandwich is called a tuna fish sandwich. Ask a grownup to help you prepare tuna fish sandwiches for everyone in your home. Before you eat, say a prayer thanking God for the food.

God is great.
God is good.
Let us thank Him
For our food.
—Traditional

While you eat the sandwiches, tell them the story of how Jesus fed more than 5,000 people.

Prayer
Dear Lord, I want to help others. Please show me ways that I can be helpful. Amen.

Don't Be Afraid

I go to bed and sleep in peace. Lord, only you keep me safe.
—PSALM 4:8

What makes you afraid? Strange noises? Dark rooms? New places?
Everyone is afraid of something. In today's Bible story, we'll even see how
Jesus' helpers were afraid. But did you know that most of the things we
are afraid of are not real or don't happen, like when we find out a strange
noise was only a tree limb scraping the side of the house? Below is a
Bible verse that you can memorize and say the next time you are afraid.

When I am afraid,
I will trust you.
—Psalm 56:3

Bible Story

Mark 6:45–53

One day Jesus asked His helpers to go to a town across the lake. He said He would join them later. The men did as Jesus asked and got into a boat and set out across the lake. A strong wind came up. The wind blew fiercely. The men were very afraid! They rowed harder and harder toward the shore, but the wind kept pushing them back into the lake. Then they saw something that scared them even more. A man was walking on the water toward them! Then the man called out, "Don't be afraid." And they realized it was Jesus walking toward them. Jesus got into their boat, and suddenly the wind became calm. The helpers were amazed. Everything was all right because Jesus was with them.

Read and Share Together

Let's Talk about It!

* ★ What made Jesus' helpers afraid?
* ★ What did Jesus do?

Share God's Love

Did you know that the Bible mentions fear more than 350 times? That's a lot of being scared. But the important thing to realize is that we know Jesus is always close by no matter what is happening.

> ### FOR FUN, ACT OUT THE STORY
>
> With your family, act out the story of the men in the boat and Jesus walking to them on the water. Pretend the floor or ground is water. The boat could be made of pillows or chairs. When you have finished your play, all together say Psalm 56:3, "When I am afraid, I will trust you." Give everyone a hug.

Prayer

Dear Lord, sometimes I am afraid. Help me know that You are always with me and to ask for Your help when I'm afraid. Amen.

Jesus Loves Me!

Jesus said, "Let the little children come to me." —MATTHEW 19:14

Isn't it good to know Jesus loves you! He loves all children. Do you know how we know? There's a hint in this song. Let's sing it together.

JESUS LOVES ME!

Jesus loves me! This I know,
For the Bible tells me so.
Little ones to Him belong;
They are weak, but He is strong.

Jesus loves me! This I know,
As He loved so long ago,
Taking children on His knee,
Saying, "Let them come to Me."

Yes, Jesus loves me!
Yes, Jesus loves me!
Yes, Jesus loves me!
The Bible tells me so.

567

Matthew 19:13–15; Mark 10:13–16; Luke 18:15–17

So many people wanted to see Jesus that they were squishing Him. There were sick people and sad people and well people and happy people, and there were people who brought their children to meet Jesus.

"No children," Jesus' helpers said to the people. "Jesus doesn't have time for them."

Jesus heard what His helpers said. He stopped them right there. "Let the little children come to Me," Jesus said, and He began to bless the children.

Children are important to God. Children are important to Jesus. He loves them. He loves you!

Let's Talk about It!

★ Why did Jesus' helpers want to send the children away?
★ What did Jesus say to His helpers?
★ How do you know Jesus loves you?

Share God's Love

Did you know that when you show kindness to others you share Jesus' love? There are lots of ways you can show kindness to others. You show kindness when you

❖ help someone,
❖ listen to someone,
❖ invite someone to play with you.

Draw a picture of one way you can show Jesus' love to others.

Prayer

Dear Jesus, thank You for loving me so much. I love You too. Amen.

God's Surprises

Come and see what the Lord has done. He has done amazing things on the earth. —Psalm 46:8

What are some of your favorite surprises? A new toy? A trip to the zoo? One of the most exciting things about God is that we never know what wonderful thing He's going to do next. It's His surprise to us. Now let's read together how God surprised Sammy. Then check out the Bible story to see how God surprised the apostle Peter.

Sammy was sad. Grandpa had been sick for a long time now. Sammy missed Grandpa's visits and the walks they used to take—just the two of them. The shelf in Sammy's room was filled with treasures he and Grandpa had found— feathers, shells, unusual rocks, and a stick that looked like an S for "Sammy." Grandpa called them God's surprises.

Just then Sammy heard three knocks, then the doorbell. It was Grandpa's special knock. Sammy dashed to the front door. "Grandpa, you're the best one of God's surprises ever!"

Bible Story

Matthew 17:24–27

When Jesus lived on earth, He paid taxes, just as people do today. One day His friend Peter came to tell Jesus they didn't have any money to pay their taxes. That didn't bother Jesus at all.

"Go fishing, Peter. You will catch a fish, and there will be a coin in its mouth. Use that to pay our taxes."

Peter had been fishing all his life, and surely he had *never* once found a coin in a fish's mouth. But he trusted Jesus. Soon Peter caught a fish, and it had a coin in its mouth. Peter used the money to pay their taxes.

Read and Share Together

Let's Talk about It!
★ What did Jesus and Peter need?
★ What did Jesus tell Peter to do?
★ What big surprise did Peter get?

Share God's Love
Peter must have looked very surprised when he saw the coin in the fish's mouth. How do you look when you're surprised? Make your most surprised look in a mirror to see. Did it make you laugh?

> ### SURPRISE!
>
> For some more fun, have everyone in your family take turns looking surprised. Then have everyone look their most surprised when you say, "One, two, three, surprise!" while someone takes a picture. When you show the picture to others, tell them about God's surprises.

Prayer
Dear Jesus, thank You for sharing Your love with me and giving me what I need. I love You. Amen.

574

Jesus Heals

The Lord says, ". . . I will lead the blind along a way they never knew. . . . I will make the darkness become light for them." —ISAIAH 42:16

Being blind means you can't see anything. People who are blind learn special skills to help them do everyday tasks. Sometimes they have a guide dog that helps them or they might carry a long white stick with a red tip to help them know when to step up or down or go around something. The stick also helps others know the person is blind.

Helen Keller was a well-known writer and speaker who was blind and deaf. She once said, "There is no better way to thank God for your sight than by giving a helping hand to someone in the dark."

575

Bible Story

Mark 10:46–52

Jesus can do anything! He can heal sick people, and He can make blind people able to see again.

One day a crowd of people was following Jesus. A blind man, who was sitting by the road, kept calling out, "Jesus, please help me!" He was so loud that some of the crowd told him to be quiet.

Jesus ignored the crowd. He asked the blind man, "What would you like Me to do for you?"

The blind man said, "I want to see."

Jesus said, "You are healed because you believe." Now the man could see.

577

Read and Share Together

Let's Talk about It!
★ What did Jesus ask the blind man?
★ What did Jesus do for the blind man?

Share God's Love
Share with your family or friends the story of how Jesus helped the blind man. Then to better understand how difficult it can be to be blind, try this experiment.

WHAT IS IT?

You'll need a bag and a blindfold. With a grownup's help, someone chooses small everyday objects—such as a rock, pencils, erasers, soap, toys, clothing, books—and places them in a bag. (No one who will be blindfolded should know what objects are in the bag.) Next the blindfolded person reaches into the bag and takes out one object. He or she has one minute to tell what the object is. Then it's someone else's turn to be blindfolded.

Prayer
Dear Lord, please help those who cannot see. Amen.

Be a Happy Giver

God loves the person who gives happily. —2 CORINTHIANS 9:7

Did you know that God wants us to give back to Him some of what He has blessed us with? Now you may be saying, "I'm just a kid. I don't have much money." Guess what? Money isn't the only way to give back to God. There are all kinds of ways to give, and the important thing is to do it with a happy heart.

Josh's friend Aaron had outgrown his winter coat, and there was no money for a new coat. Josh had a great idea. He would wear his big brother's old coat and give his own coat to Aaron. Mom, Dad, Josh's brother, Aaron, and Jesus liked Josh's "happy-giver" plan!

Mark 12:41–44

Jesus watched as people put their money in an offering box at the Temple. The rich people were giving a lot of money.

But then, from the back of the crowd came a very poor woman. She dropped her two copper coins into the box.

When Jesus saw her, He said to His followers, "This woman gave more than the rich people with many coins. She gave all the money she had."

Read and Share Together

Let's Talk about It!
* Who gave a lot of money?
* Who gave all she had?
* What did Jesus say about her gift?

Share God's Love

God can do great things with the small things you give, whether it is giving a small coin or a few hours of your time. Giving your time to help others is called volunteering, and it's a good way to give back to God. Ask your parents what your family can do to help others in your community. Maybe you can get your church involved by starting a contest in your Sunday school class. Divide the class into two teams and see which team can collect the most canned food for hungry families in your community.

Prayer

Dear Lord, help me to give with a happy heart.
Thank You for blessing me in so many ways. Amen.

Mighty Jesus!

I asked the Lord for help, and he answered me.
He saved me from all that I feared. —Psalm 34:4

Did you know that clouds can tell us a lot about the weather? But even if we learn everything about clouds, we still cannot control clouds or the weather. Only God and Jesus can do that. Check out today's Bible story and see what a mighty thing Jesus did. The next time you are outside, see if you can find any of the clouds listed below:

1. *Cirrus* clouds are high, thin wispy clouds that look like a horse's tail. These clouds don't give us a clue about the weather.
2. *Cirrocumulus* clouds are rows of white clouds sailing across the sky. They mean tomorrow's weather will be good.
3. *Nimbostratus* clouds are dark gray rain clouds. These clouds mean: get out your umbrella.
4. *Cumulonimbus* are "thunderhead" clouds. They have a flat base and a tall middle. These usually mean rain, thunder, lightning, and hail.

Mark 4:35–41

One day after Jesus had been teaching all day long, He and His friends got into a boat to go across the lake. Jesus was so tired He fell asleep. Before His friends could row across the lake, up came a strong storm. The wind began to whip around. Waves splashed high against the boat and began to fill it with water. It was a scary time.

Finally, Jesus' friends woke Him up. They were afraid. "Help us, or we'll drown!" they said. Jesus stood up and instead of grabbing an oar to help row, He spoke to the storm. "Quiet! Be still!" Jesus said. The wind stopped. The waves calmed down, and everyone was safe. Jesus is so mighty the wind and waves obey Him!

Read and Share Together

Let's Talk about It!
★ What did Jesus do when He got into the boat?
★ What happened next?
★ What did Jesus say to the storm?

Share God's Love
Jesus is mighty. He made the storm stop as easy as turning on a light. If you were to crawl under a blanket, it would be dark and maybe a little scary. But if you were to turn on a flashlight under the blanket, it wouldn't be so scary. Try it and see. And the next time you and your family or friends are looking at the clouds, tell them how Jesus stopped a storm.

Prayer
Dear Lord, You are so mighty You can do anything. Thank You for being with me all the time—in stormy and sunny weather. Amen.

The Good Shepherd

"I am the good shepherd. The good shepherd gives his life for the sheep." —JOHN 10:11

Have you ever been to a zoo or farm where keepers care for sheep? In our time together today, we're going to see how a shepherd takes care of his sheep when they wander off. Jesus is called our Good Shepherd. Sometimes we are like sheep. We wander off. We get in trouble. We forget to follow Jesus who takes care of us as a shepherd takes care of his sheep. Psalm 23 in the Bible tells how the Lord is our Shepherd. Below is how it begins. Ask someone to help you find it and read the rest in your Bible.

The Lord is my shepherd.
I have everything I need.
He gives me rest in green pastures.
He leads me to calm water.
He gives me new strength.
—Psalm 23 (excerpt)

Bible Story

Luke 15:3–7

Jesus told a story about a shepherd who had 100 sheep. Every night when the shepherd brought his sheep home he counted them to make sure they were all there.

One night after he counted 99 sheep, there were no more sheep to count. One sheep was missing. The shepherd left his 99 sheep safe at home and went right out to find the one lost sheep. He looked high. He looked low. He looked everywhere. And finally he found the sheep.

The happy shepherd put the sheep on his shoulders—that's the way shepherds used to carry their sheep—and brought it home. The shepherd was so happy that he had a party with his friends to celebrate finding his lost sheep.

Read and Share Together

Let's Talk about It!
* ★ Who is the Good Shepherd?
* ★ What did the shepherd do every night?
* ★ What did he do when he found one sheep missing?

Share God's Love

Doesn't it make you feel good to know that Jesus takes care of us just like the shepherd took care of his sheep! A fun game to help you remember that Jesus is our Good Shepherd, and that we need to follow Him in all that we do, is Follow the Shepherd.

FOLLOW THE SHEPHERD

Choose a shepherd, then stand in a line behind the shepherd. The shepherd says, "Follow me!" and then does an action like raise his or her hands or walk backward. Everyone must do exactly what the shepherd does. After the shepherd does three different things, he or she goes to the end of the line and the person in the front of the line is the shepherd. When everyone has had a turn, clap hands and start again.

Prayer

Dear Jesus, I'm so glad You care about me. Thank You for coming to search for me when I wander off in my heart and forget to follow You. Help me to love and obey You. Amen.

Forgiven

"Everyone who believes in Jesus will be forgiven.
God will forgive his sins through Jesus." —Acts 10:43

Have you done or said something you knew was not right? Jamie did . . .

Jamie knew it was against the rules to toss his football in the house, but he did it anyway. Uh-oh, it hit the wall and . . . *CRASH!* Jamie's mother came running into the room.

"Mom, I broke your lamp. I'm sorry. Can you forgive me?" Jamie asked.

"Yes," she said. "But there will be consequences for breaking the rules. I'll keep your football for two days." Jamie helped clean up the mess. Then his mother gave him a big hug.

Here's some really great news! No matter how naughty we have been, God will forgive us if we ask Him.

Luke 15:11–24

There was a man who had two sons. The younger son decided he wanted the money that would be his when his father died while his father was alive. His father gave him the money. The son went off to another country and spent all his money on foolish things. After his money was gone, the son was hungry and alone. He got a job feeding pigs, and he was so hungry he even thought about eating the pigs' food.

Then he realized that his father's servants had more food than he had. He decided to go home, tell his father he was sorry, and ask if he could just be a servant. And that's what he did. To his surprise, when he went home, his father gave him a big hug and forgave him for all he had done.

Read and Share Together

Let's Talk about It!

★ What did the younger son ask from his father?
★ What happened to the younger son's money?
★ When the younger son came home, what did his father do?

Share God's Love

Yuck! Can you imagine being so hungry that you would consider eating pig food? But isn't it comforting to know that if we mess up like the son in the Bible story, we can ask God, our heavenly Father, to forgive us and He will? He's like the father in the Bible story. He accepts us as we are when we ask for forgiveness.

Have you done something wrong? Talk to God right now and tell Him you are sorry. Ask Him to forgive you. And remember God wants you to forgive others just like He forgives you.

Prayer

Dear Lord, I ask You to forgive me for the wrongs I have done. Help me to do what is right. Amen.

When Jesus Cried

Jesus cried. —JOHN 11:35

Have you ever been sad when someone you loved died? Well, Jesus knows how sad it makes us feel when those we love die. He knows because He felt the same way when His friend Lazarus died. The Bible tells us that when Lazarus died, Jesus was so sad He cried. It's okay to be sad, and even to cry, but here's a happy thought to remember: some day we'll see our loved ones again in heaven. Till then we can remember the good times we had with them. And when those happy memories make us smile, that's okay too.

Tear drops fall like the rain
When our hearts are sad.
Jesus sees each tear that falls.
He makes sad hearts glad.
—Gwen Ellis

John 11:1–44

Jesus loved His friends Martha, Mary, and Lazarus.
One day when Jesus was away, Lazarus became ill.
When Jesus heard His friend was ill, Jesus waited
two days to start His trip to see His friends.
By the time Jesus arrived, Lazarus had been
dead for four days. Lazarus' sister Mary said,
"Jesus, if You had been here, my brother
would not have died." Jesus was so sad,
He cried. Then Jesus walked to Lazarus'
tomb and asked the people there to
move the stone from the entrance.

In a loud voice Jesus said, "Lazarus, come out!" And out of the tomb walked Lazarus, all wrapped up in burial clothes! He was alive and well.

Read and Share Together

Let's Talk about It!

★ Who became ill?
★ What did Jesus do when He heard His friend Lazarus had died?
★ What happened next?

Share God's Love

Were you surprised to learn that Jesus cried? What makes you sad? When friends are happy, it's easy to share their joy. But when friends are sad, it's hard to share their sorrow. Did you know you can help your friends through sad times by doing some very simple things to let them know you care:

✤ Take them cookies you helped bake.
✤ Listen to them.
✤ Be kind to them.
✤ Sit quietly next to them.
✤ Pray with them and for them.

And if you are the one who is sad—tell a grownup, talk to Jesus, and allow your friends to comfort you.

Prayer

Dear Lord, I know it's okay to be sad sometimes. Thank You for the happy memories I have of those who have gone to heaven to be with You. Amen.

A Thankful Heart

Thank the Lord because he is good. His love continues forever.
—PSALM 107:1

Has anyone ever thanked you for something you gave or did for him or her? How did it make you feel? The good thing about the words "thank you" is that they make both the one saying them and the one they're said to feel good. God wants you to have a thankful heart like the man in the Bible story we are going to read on the next page. Right now, practice having a thankful heart by playing the Thank-You Game.

THE THANK-YOU GAME

Put a lot of squares of different colored paper in a bag. Then pull out a piece and give thanks for something that color. For example: If the paper is white, what you might be thankful for is milk or snow. Green might be for grass or a favorite shirt.

Luke 17:11–19

One day Jesus was walking along a road when He saw ten men. They did not come close to Jesus because they had a skin disease called leprosy. The men called out to Jesus, "Please help us." Jesus healed all ten men. As they went on their way, the sores and bumps on their skin went away—which meant that their skin disease disappeared. They were well.

When one of the ten men saw that his skin was healed, he turned around and hurried back to thank Jesus for healing him. But he was the only one to say, "Thank you." He had a thankful heart.

Read and Share Together

Let's Talk about It!
★ What was wrong with the ten men in the story?
★ What did they ask Jesus to do?
★ How many men said thank you?

Share God's Love
When you thank others for what they do for you, then you have a thankful heart. To share God's love with your family, here's a fun thing to do.

As fast as you can, say all the things you're thankful for about each member of your family.

You may also want to make a list of these to use when you say your prayers. When you say your prayers, name each person and say what you are thankful for about that person.

Prayer
Dear Lord, thank You for my family. Here are some things I'm thankful for about each person in my family . . . Amen.

Let Me Serve You

When we have the opportunity to help anyone,
we should do it. —GALATIANS 6:10

"May I help you?" Where have you heard these words? From a server in a restaurant or a clerk in a store? But did you know that Jesus wants us all to find ways to serve one another? Not because it's a job, but because we have kind and loving hearts and think of others.

Here's a fun way to practice serving others. Offer to be the server at dinner. As the server, you should tell those being served what foods are available. After each person chooses what he or she would like to eat, write down their order and go get the food for them.

John 13:1–17

During Jesus' last days on earth, He and His closest followers had an evening meal together. It was the time of the Jewish Passover Feast. During their meal, Jesus got up from the table, took off His coat, wrapped a towel around His waist, and poured water into a big bowl.

Then He went from one of His friends to the next washing their dusty, maybe even smelly, feet.

He did this to show them how to serve one another. If Jesus, their leader, could act as their servant and wash their feet, they could do things to help and serve others too.

Read and Share Together

Let's Talk about It!
★ What were Jesus and His followers doing?
★ During dinner, what did Jesus do?

Share God's Love
What are some ways you can serve others at home, at church, and at school? Following are some ideas, but there's a trick. Can you find the one idea that is *not* a way to serve others?

1. Rake the leaves in your grandma's yard.
2. Eat a piece of chocolate cake.
3. Give the clothes you've outgrown to someone who needs them.
4. Offer to help feed your neighbor's dog while they're on vacation.

(Did you guess number two is not a way to serve others? If so, you're right, and well on your way to serving others.)

Prayer
Dear Lord, if You can be a servant to others, so can I.
Help me find ways to serve others. Amen.

Happy Easter!

"God raised Jesus from death." —Acts 13:34

Beautiful Easter eggs and cute bunny rabbits! Is that what you think about first when you think of Easter? Guess what . . . the celebration of Easter is about something much more important. It's the day many Christians celebrate Jesus rising from death. That's right! Jesus came back to life to show that He is our Savior, and if we believe in Him, when we die we'll live with Him in heaven.

He arose! He arose!
Hallelujah! Christ arose!
—Robert Lowry (1874)
   Excerpt from "Up from the Grave He Arose"

Matthew 27–28:10

After Jesus died on the Cross, His friends were very sad. They placed His body inside a tomb. Then they rolled a large heavy stone over it. Roman soldiers came, sealed the stone opening, and stood guard at the tomb.

On the third day after Jesus had died, some women went to His tomb. When they got there, they couldn't believe their eyes. The stone had been rolled away, and an angel of God was sitting on top of it. The tomb was empty. The angel said, "Don't be afraid. Jesus is alive. Tell His followers they'll see Him in Galilee." The women hurried to tell the others the good news—Jesus is alive!

Read and Share Together

Let's Talk about It!
★ What happened to Jesus on the Cross?
★ Where did the women go?
★ What did the angel say?

Share God's Love
Aren't you glad Jesus rose from death to be our Savior so we can live with Him in heaven some day! Here's a fun way to celebrate Jesus coming back to life—even if it is not near Easter when you read this. Ask a grownup to boil some eggs and help you dye them. Before dipping the eggs in the dye, write on each one in crayon the name of the person you want to have the egg. When the eggs are dry, give each person the egg with his or her name on it, then say, "Hallelujah, Jesus is alive!"

EASTER EGG DYE

To make an Easter egg dye, put about 1/4 teaspoon food coloring in 3/4 cup of hot water. Then add 1 tablespoon of white vinegar to the water and stir.

Prayer
Dear Lord, I am so glad You are alive. Thank You
for making it possible for me to go to heaven. Amen.

610

Good News!

"How beautiful is the person who comes to bring good news."
—ROMANS 10:15

What kind of news did you hear today? Was it good news? Was it not-so-good news? For fun, tell which of the following news flashes is good (G) and which is bad (B). See the answers below.

NEWS FLASHES

1. A storm blew the roof off our house.
2. Today we built a snowman.
3. Our dog has four new puppies.
4. Jodi has a sore throat.

[1. B / 2. G / 3. G / 4. B]

Now here's the very best news the world ever heard: Jesus is God's Son, and He died to save us from sin. When we tell others about Jesus, we are sharing the Good News.

Acts 8:26–40

Philip was one of Jesus' followers who liked to tell people the Good News about Jesus. One day an angel spoke to Philip and told him to go to the desert road. On the road an important man from Ethiopia rode by in his chariot, reading the book of Isaiah. Philip ran alongside the chariot and asked if the man understood what he was reading.

The man said no, and asked Philip to explain it to him. Philip told him the Good News about Jesus. The man from Ethiopia believed what Philip told him and asked Philip to baptize him. After baptizing the man, Philip went to tell others the Good News.

Read and Share Together

Let's Talk about It!
* ★ What did Philip tell the man from Ethiopia?
* ★ What did the man from Ethiopia ask Philip?

Share God's Love
Philip shared the Good News about Jesus, and you can too. Here's a fun way to practice.

TELLING THE GOOD NEWS

With a microphone, pretend to be a TV newsperson and in your own words tell the Good News about Jesus to your family and friends. Be sure and tell the whole story of how Jesus was sent by God to save us from our sins, and how Jesus died on the Cross, was buried, and came to life again so that we could have a home in heaven when we die.

Prayer
Dear Lord, I want to share Your Good News with everyone! Amen.

A Life That Shines

Christ himself died for you. And that one death
paid for your sins. —1 PETER 3:18

Have you ever told anyone about Jesus? How He's God's Son who died
to save us from our sin? Jesus wants us to tell others that He loves them
and will save them too. We can also show others how Jesus loves them
just by the way we act. When we live a life that's pleasing to God by
treating others with kindness, we're like a light shining in the darkness
to show them the way to Jesus.

A CHILD'S PRAYER

God make my life a little light,
  Within the world to glow;
A tiny flame that burns so bright
  Wherever I may go.
—M. Betham-Edwards

615

Acts 16:12–15

After Paul became a follower of Jesus, he went everywhere telling people the Good News about Jesus: How Jesus was God's Son, and how He died on the Cross for our sins.

One day Paul met a woman named Lydia. Her job was selling purple cloth. She loved God, but she didn't know about Jesus.

When Paul told Lydia who Jesus was and what He had done for her, she believed what Paul said and was baptized. All the people in her house believed and were baptized too.

Read and Share Together

Let's Talk about It!
★ Why did Jesus die on the Cross?
★ How can we help others know this Good News?

Share God's Love
The news about Jesus saving us from our sin is too good to keep to ourselves. For a fun way to share the news, make a picture book to show your friends and family when you tell them about Jesus.

> **Page 1:** Draw a person with a sad face and a dark, dirty heart. This page stands for a person's heart before Jesus comes into it. They are dark with sin.
> **Page 2:** Draw a red cross. The red cross is for Jesus dying for our sins.
> **Page 3:** Draw a person with a clean heart. When we receive Jesus into our hearts, He takes away all the darkness and gives us a heart that is clean and new.
> **Page 4:** Draw a picture of a house using a yellow-gold crayon. The house stands for the mansion in heaven Jesus is making for all who believe in Him.

Prayer
Dear Lord, I believe You are God's Son. Thank You for dying for me so that I can someday live in heaven with You and God. Amen.

When It's Not Funny to Laugh

Do not let my enemies laugh at me. —PSALM 35:19

Sometimes when people laugh, it's not so good. Has anyone ever laughed at you when you weren't trying to be funny? If so, how did it make you feel? Not good, right? Did you know that God understands how we feel when we are laughed at or called names? It makes Him sad. Even the apostle Paul was laughed at because people didn't believe what he was saying about Jesus. In today's Bible story, find out why people laughed at Paul.

I laughed when my sister
fell down the stair.
I called her a clumsy teddy bear.

When baby brother
wrecked his sled,
I laughed and laughed 'til I turned red.

Then one day,
I slipped in the mud.
I went down with a great big
*   THUD!*

My friends wiggled and giggled
*   and pointed, you see.*
It wasn't any fun when they
*   laughed at me.*

—June Ford

619

Acts 17:16–34

The apostle Paul was a preacher who traveled all over telling people the Good News about Jesus. One day he was in the capital city of Greece—Athens. There was a place in Athens called Mars Hill. Men went there to talk to each other and to argue about everything. Paul saw an altar they had built. Written on it were the words "To the God who is not known."

Well, Paul began to tell them about our God and how He raised Jesus from death. Paul told them that they could know God too. Some of the people began to laugh at Paul. They were not ready to believe in God, and Paul could not change their minds.

Read and Share Together

Let's Talk about It!
* Who was Paul?
* What did Paul tell the people about the "God who is not known"?
* Why did some of the people laugh at Paul?

Share God's Love
Have you ever been like the people who laughed at Paul, laughing because you didn't believe someone? How would you feel if you found out what the person was saying was true? How would you feel if you were Paul and being laughed at? Tell a story about when laughter is not a good thing, like when someone laughs in a mean way. Now tell a story about when laughter is a happy thing.

Prayer
Dear Lord, You know that bullies do mean things.
Help them learn to be kind. Amen.

A Sudden Storm

All you who put your hope in the Lord be strong and brave.
—PSALM 31:24

When we have hope, we believe things will turn out for the best. God gives us hope because He is always doing what is best for us, and wanting us to do our best. And we have hope because we trust in God.

Twins Chester and Charlotte stood inside the school lobby watching as a cold wind whirled snowflakes outside. A sudden snowstorm had caught them unprepared for the walk home.

"We'd better go before the weather gets worse," Chester said.

"I still hope he'll come," Charlotte said. "I just know he will."

Just then the door swung open, and there stood the twins' dad holding their warm winter coats, hats, gloves, and boots. "Anyone need a ride home?"

623

Bible Story

Acts 27

Paul, the apostle, got on a big ship headed for Rome, Italy. After a time at sea, a strong wind came up and blew hard against the sails of the ship. The storm was so bad that the people on the ship lost all hope of staying alive. They thought they would die. But God sent an angel to tell Paul that all who sailed with him would be saved, but the ship would crash and be lost. Paul told them what God had said. He knew God would keep His promise. That gave everyone on the ship a great deal of hope. They weren't so frightened. When morning came, the ship hit a sandbank near an island and broke apart. Everyone who couldn't swim grabbed something that would float, like a piece of wood, and made it to the island's shore. They were all saved.

Read and Share Together

Let's Talk about It!
★ Where was the apostle Paul going on the ship?
★ What happened on the way?

Share God's Love
Isn't God awesome! There were 276 people on-board the ship Paul was on and all of them survived the shipwreck. If you had been on that ship with Paul, how would you have felt when he told them they would not die?

> ### FOR FUN, ACT OUT THE STORY
>
> Use something like a blanket, sheet, string, or garden hose to make the shape of a boat. Put things such as pillows, boxes, and baskets in the boat. Choose something like an outside wall or the back of a sofa to be the island's shore. Choose one person to be Paul. The rest of the family can be the sailors and other passengers on the ship. Get inside the boat, and as someone reads the Bible story, act it out.

Prayer
Dear Lord, please help me to always have hope and to know that You are stronger than anything that can happen in my life. Amen.

A Home in Heaven

"No one has ever imagined what God has prepared for those who love him." —1 Corinthians 2:9

Jesus made many promises, but the best is yet to come. He said He would have a special place ready for us when our lives on earth are over. That place is called heaven, and it's more beautiful than anything we've ever seen. It's so beautiful that if you were to draw a picture of what you think heaven might look like, you'd probably need to use all the colors in your crayon box. Think of an entire city made of gold and every kind of precious jewels, like green emeralds and blue sapphires and purple amethysts. Think of streets made of gold and gates made of pearl.

Well, heaven is like that. And it's a place without pain or sadness or death. And best of all, Jesus will be there. We will be with Him forever.

John 14:1–2; Revelation 21

One day Jesus talked with His friends and followers about heaven. He said, "Don't let your hearts be troubled. Trust in God. And trust in Me. There are many rooms in My Father's house. I would not tell you this if it were not true. I am going there to prepare a place for you."

God promises that in heaven no one will ever be sad again. No one will ever be sick again. Everything will be more wonderful than we have ever imagined. And we will be happy there forever.

Read and Share Together

Let's Talk about It!
* What did Jesus say He was going to do for us in heaven?
* Will we be sad in heaven?
* What's the best part of heaven?

Share God's Love
Wow! How wonderful it is to have heaven to look forward to!
Here are some things that will help you think about how
wonderful heaven will be:

1. Tell about the most beautiful place you have ever seen.
   (Heaven will be a thousand times more beautiful.)
2. Make up your own song about how wonderful heaven
   will be.

Prayer
*Dear Lord, thank You for Your promise of heaven. I know
You have lots of things for me to do first in this life. But it's
so good to know You have a place waiting for me. Amen.*

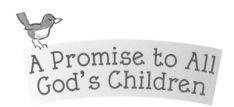

A Promise to All God's Children

"No one has ever seen this.
No one has ever heard about it.
No one has ever imagined
what God has prepared
for those who love him."

1 Corinthians 2:9

Bringing the Bible to life for your little ones with **Read and Share**®

Packed with 200 stories, the *Read and Share® Bible* is sure to win the hearts of little ones and give them a strong Bible foundation.

The *Read and Share® Toddler Bible* offers 40 stories plus a 60-minute DVD for even the littlest of God's children.

The *Read and Share® Devotional* offers 52 devotions based on the Read and Share® Bible, packed with fun activities to help children learn about God's love

The *Read and Share® DVD Bible* series builds a foundation in knowing God's Word in young minds. Collection includes 52, 3-minute Bible stories in bold, bright animation.

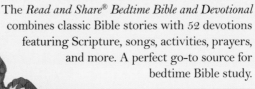

Straight from the pages of the popular *Read and Share® Bible*, The Jesus Series walks children though the birth, life, death and resurrection of Christ.

The *Read and Share® Bedtime Bible and Devotional* combines classic Bible stories with 52 devotions featuring Scripture, songs, activities, prayers, and more. A perfect go-to source for bedtime Bible study.

Learn more about *Read and Share®!*
www.tommynelson.com